GROWING UP
PUERTO RICAN

GROWING UP PUERTO RICAN

EDITED BY
PAULETTE COOPER

with a Foreword by
JOSÉ TORRES

ARBOR HOUSE
NEW YORK

To Dr. Stanley Cath

CONTENTS

8   *CONTENTS*

FOREWORD

When I was a kid, growing up in Ponce, Puerto Rico, I was told not to talk, but to listen. It was an era of proud, vain men, and docile, submissive women. It was *machismo* at its peak. I and many of my friends were twelve when we first found out that the Three Wise Men were in reality our parents. Confronted with this reality, we cried. At eleven, and some of us, even at fifteen, were still chicken.

Today, this is no longer true. Today the children are aware of situations which affect their lives; they are mixed up in everything that in the past was considered adult stuff. This book is about them, about today's Puerto Ricans and their experiences, about their struggles, frustrations, and hopes.

My childhood was filled with naivete and innocence. We kids were more interested in playing children's games than in playing with sex. Perhaps this is why I am so fascinated by today's Puerto Rican youth, both here and in Puerto Rico.

It is interesting that this book seems to have a grasp on something that I don't find in books written by Puerto Ricans. Perhaps the fact that the editor, Paulette Cooper, is not a Puerto Rican is an advantage. I, for one, would have taken for granted many of the little, yet important things that this book illuminates.

The interviews she reports have showed me that we Puerto Ricans are still searching for identity in a strange place. Perhaps that's why one can find Puerto Ricans on the island who will tell you that Puerto Rico should become a state of the U. S., while Puerto Ricans here, especially those who have never been in Puerto Rico, would even kill for the freedom of Puerto Rico.

Sociologists deal with abstractions. But this book has the words of the people themselves, people of varying status and environment. Unlike Oscar Lewis' *La Vida,* which dealt with one small segment of *one* Puerto Rican family, this book covers Puerto Ricans from many different social strata. Yet there are fascinating similarities: the husband hits his wife; there are experiences with drugs; sex at an early age; most of those interviewed come from broken homes, and share the hopes to go back to Puerto Rico.

I see in the book, too, the basis for *our* generation gap. Most of the Puerto Ricans who speak of it did not come here by their own choosing. They were brought here by their mothers or fathers.

These Puerto Ricans interviewed by Miss Cooper were in effect taken out of the house with the big yard, the beautiful scenery, the hospital people, and the good weather. And they were brought to rat- and roach-infested, dilapidated buildings, to a place which is too cold in the winter and too hot in the summer.

Their parents did this to them, and they simply rebel—although they are very much of this country, something in them also wants to go home. And yet as things improve for them, hopefully this will become a happy home for them, and one in which they too will be proud to have their children grow up.

José Torres

INTRODUCTION

GROWING UP IS never an easy process for anyone, whether he's brought up in a ghetto shack or an elegant mansion in the most exclusive part of town. But the growing up process is a far more painful experience when, by an accident of birth, someone is born a member of an outcast minority group. His whole infancy is spent struggling for survival; his entire childhood is devoted to fighting for an opportunity to be treated as equal; and all his adult years are spent trying to recover from society's unforgettable early blows.

I know from my own experience, for while I was not born as a Puerto Rican in America, I was born as a Jew in Belgium toward the end of World War II. As a result, I almost didn't live to grow up at all. By the time I was born, my father had already been killed by Hitler for absolutely no reason other than that he was a Jew in Belgium at the wrong time. And my mother underwent the same fate as my father (for the same non-reason) a few months after she gave birth to me. I did my growing up in a Belgian orphanage, and can therefore understand the loneliness and unhappiness of the early childhood of many of the people I interviewed for this book.

But unlike most of them here, I was given a second chance. I was taken out of the orphanage at the age of six and adopted by the most marvelous American couple. They gave me everything I had never had as a very young child: love, warmth and understanding. They also gave me the chance to learn what it was like to have physical as well as emotional comfort, and I must admit that the fact that, in the neighborhood in which we lived, I was no longer a member of an outcast minority group was a comfort to me. They also helped me to accomplish what I wanted to do in life by sending me to college and then graduate school. In both places I studied psychology (perhaps not surprisingly, specializing in clinical child psychology), and did my master's thesis on early childhood memories.

Therefore my interest in the problems of these young people I interviewed is more than just journalistic. I found it very easy to identify with many of them—especially the girl who spent most of her years in an orphanage. I found as I interviewed them that at times I was getting very emotionally involved, even occasionally fighting back tears. I was aware that it was probably wrong journalistically, although, for this book, it may have helped by making them feel more comfortable with me. Many of these people had never before felt that anyone was moved by them because no one had ever listened to them before. But regardless of whether I should or shouldn't have gotten involved, as a human being who had undergone some similar early experiences, I found it unavoidable. Ultimately though, the whole experience changed me as a person. Listening to them not only helped me by teaching me about Puerto Ricans, whom I had never known before, but it helped me by teaching me something about *me*, whom I had never known before. My early problems were not that unique, and if other people could survive with and through similar experiences and memories, then so could and would I.

None of the people in this book were lucky enough to go from hell to heaven as I did. In fact, many of them took the exact opposite trip. A large number of them were uprooted from a warm, friendly country—Puerto Rico—into a cold hostile environment—America. Several of them lived in large houses in Puerto Rico with backyards and open spaces, and then came here where the exhorbitant rents and deplorable lack of space in our ghettos forced them into tiny cramped quarters where they had to share rooms and bed and blankets. It was sad to hear many of them talk about how beautiful life had been for them in Puerto Rico, in contrast to the "hassle" it became in America. Many of these people were literally taken out of heaven, and this vision of an earthly paradise in which they once lived, along with the realization that they will never again return there, only deepens their unhappiness and despair.

There are so many other special problems that Puerto Ricans face today and that they describe in these interviews. But, as you read their stories, I hope you will notice, as I did, that despite all their problems, Puerto Ricans are a warm and generous people who have managed to keep their sanity and sense of humor despite all that has been done to them. Fernanda, who now has a master's degree, was told in grade school that she had an I.Q. of 73. Mario, who's half black and half Puerto Rican, was consistently denounced for being both. Carmelita was almost killed by a drug addict. Rodriguez was beaten up every day on his way to school just because he was Puerto Rican. But none of them have given up. On the contrary. I found as I talked to them a very positive sense of hope—the feeling that things will somehow get better for them. Despite all of the problems Puerto Ricans face today, many of them are beginning to see signs of change, and some are really trying to do something about it. It may be an attempt to change society, but more often, it's an attempt to find themselves. Some of them have found happiness and themselves through God; some through an affirmation of their own values and beliefs—some in their new-found pride in being Puerto Rican. As Rosita says, "Puerto Ricans are different. Good different." I saw this while researching this book; hopefully you will see it while reading it.

PAULETTE COOPER

THE WINNER

My NAME IS FERNANDA. I was born in Puerto Rico, and I was 11 years old when I came here. When I was little in Puerto Rico my father was very successful. He had his own business, he was a sales representative there for a number of American firms. He was a very political man, he had been that way since the 1930s, and he was warm, intelligent, and like many Puerto Ricans, occasionally hot-headed. He was very much involved in the *machismo* situation, and was strict and the head of the family. Although he ran our family in Puerto Rico, he never used corporal punishment because he had gone through that himself when he was a child. He had been brought up by his uncle and lived with his cousins, and if he came home late, his punishment would be to stay and work on the farm for the entire summer, or he would be horsewhipped. It wasn't that his uncle played favorites with his own sons; it was simply the way the uncle was.

My mother was a nurse, but I don't remember anything of her because she died of cancer when I was three years old. Then my godmother took care of me for the next five years. She was a loving, warm person and I was very attached to her and thought of her as my mother. I was extremely unhappy when my father remarried and I had to go to live with my father and new mother when I was seven and a half years old.

Originally she was nice, I suppose, but she was a very aggressive woman with a strong personality, and she had led a different sort of life and had very definite attitudes as to how things should be. And everybody had to adjust to her. Unfortunately there was a lot of conflict between her and my father because he also had definite ideas of how things should be, and they quarreled a lot. One of the main sources of friction was that she wanted to work and he didn't want her to. She didn't have to for financial reasons, but she was not overly fond of house-cleaning and caring for me, and I suppose she wanted to establish her own identity.

Another constant source of irritation between them was my upbringing. She wanted him to be stricter and more authoritarian, but because of his background and feelings he wanted none of that. Sometimes he used to take me aside and tell me to go along with her for the sake of peace in the family, which I did, but often the fights got far more violent than that. Four or five times things became so bad that I was sent to my godmother to live, and I was so happy. Each time I thought it meant I was leaving them and returning to the happier, more peaceful life forever. But it never lasted. Suddenly my father would show up and happily tell me that all had been patched up with my stepmother and he was taking me back home. Which he did, and I was miserable because the fighting always started again shortly thereafter.

Still, I think life in Puerto Rico was happy. Maybe all children find their earliest years happy. But back home there were always a lot of happy people at our house. Friends. Relatives. Many friends would come to visit us and I liked that. Then too we were financially comfortable. We had a big house, with lots of space for all of us, including my baby step-sister who was born there. We had a big backyard and lots of trees—all things I took for granted until we came here. I liked the warm weather in Puerto Rico, unlike the weather here. I always did well in school in Puerto Rico because my father was hung up on achievement and encouraged me to succeed. I suppose I always did what he wanted me to because he was the authority in the house regardless of all the tensions and difficulties. He was the breadwinner and experienced himself as successful in personal values and also in financial status. Which he was.

And then everything changed when we came here. He had been the import representative for equipment that was sold to large factories. But during the war there were no ships coming in to Puerto Rico because there was a blockade, so there were no active factories and no food and no buyers. Remember that in those days things weren't done by planes but by ships. So his business had folded. The American government paid for him to go back to school in Puerto Rico and study welding, and then he came to New York to work in the Navy Yard with a guarantee that his family would be here in a year. Which we were.

In 1943 my stepmother and I followed him here. But that's when things started to collapse. For one thing, my stepmother was not used to doing housework because in Puerto Rico we were rich enough and it was cheap enough always to have people work to take care of things like the cooking and my care. And being a housewife wasn't her forte. As a result, the place we lived in got very rundown. Another problem, and one I always blamed on my father although now I realize that he meant well, came from his getting an apartment in a ghetto. He wanted to be near my uncle and relatives and thought the adjustment would be easier for all of us if we lived with the family, and where they spoke Spanish. But in retrospect it was a terrible mistake. It was a ghetto area and the neighborhood was of course dreadful and dangerous. We lived in a small railroad apartment on the top floor of a tenement. All together there were five of us living there, including two infants who cried all the time.

The neighborhood to me appeared dirty and crowded, especially after the wide, open spaces of Puerto Rico and the beautiful place we had lived in. I was used to a yard and trees and a lot of freedom in terms of space. Furthermore, I had seen many movies in Puerto Rico of America —you know the big Hollywood spectaculars—and I was terribly disappointed because this was hardly the type of place you saw on the screen. And I suppose that I blamed my father, the way a child does, because of his terrible choice.

The situation between my father and stepmother had never been good, but it got really bad here. She wasn't used to being a housewife and caring for kids and this gave rise to squabbles and quarrels. They never became physical but they certainly became bitter. In Puerto Rico I could have walked out and played in the backyard and shut the things out the way a child sometimes can do. But here? In a railroad flat it was hard to miss a single fight. Listening to them fight like that was a devastating, shattering experience.

Another source of constant fighting was money. Every week when he got his pay check, there was another battle. My father claimed he brought her his whole pay check and he couldn't figure out why she hadn't saved any money—the apartment wasn't expensive—and he desperately wanted her to save enough so he could return to Puerto Rico. His dream was to go back there and start a business and be successful as he once had been. She had a lot of her family here, and he accused her of supporting them with the money she should have been saving for us. She, on the other hand, accused him of bringing home only part of his pay check and using the other part to support some of his friends. He had done that sort of thing in Puerto Rico—when his friends needed help he was always glad to oblige—and she was sure he was doing it here. They tried to draw me into the fights but I didn't want to take sides. In retrospect, I think perhaps both were right. She was probably helping her family and he was probably helping his friends.

At any rate he became terribly depressed over the change in life style, the new job and the problems with my stepmother. And all that aggravation was probably responsible for his having a very serious heart attack at the age of thirty-seven. But then something even worse happened to him. He was a very independent self-assertive man and suddenly he could no longer work. Even worse, he had always looked down on people who got welfare checks, and suddenly he was also. His pride as a father, a man and a provider were totally shattered. He couldn't even tell me about it because he had also taught me to look down on people who needed doles. But I began to guess what was happening. I had to get my teacher to sign certain things, and I saw a woman coming to our house quite regularly. He always tried to get me out of the room when she came, but you kind of pick things up. I knew she was the welfare investigator.

I became extremely agitated. Here he had always taught me that to accept handouts was a terrible thing, and I could see that now he was doing what he had criticized other people for. But I wasn't the only one who became upset. I suppose you could say that he suffered a nervous breakdown during this period. He went into a deep depression and ultimately needed psychiatric treatment. He sat in the house all day—which he had to for medical reasons—but he wouldn't shave, he wouldn't change his clothes, he wouldn't do anything. He just sat there and stared. By necessity my mother had to go to work then, and that did it as far as he was concerned. It became a great source of friction and unfortunately a weapon my stepmother could use against him—she was the breadwinner now.

He couldn't work for ten years. Although he was under doctor's orders not to, I suppose it was the proud Puerto Rican in him that made him try regardless. But the amount of work he could do and the energy he could expend were limited, and the two businesses he tried failed. This made things even worse. The roles became reversed and this proud businessman had to stay home and cook and take care of us.

Now I understand. But then, as an adolescent, I

couldn't. I was totally turned off against him. I had nothing to do with him if I could help it. And I only related to my younger sister in a motherly sort of way. Since my father wasn't functioning and my mother became the father, I became the mother. But the effect it had on me was devastating.

I had done extremely well in school until then, but by high school, when I was undergoing all this turmoil and witnessing all these events, I began to have serious problems which were not helped by being Puerto Rican. I tried to get along with the other kids but had trouble with my father who was still fiercely nationalistic and political. He didn't like me speaking English at home, or dressing in loafers, wearing buttons for Perry Como and, well, being American. He always said that I didn't have respect for my elders which I suppose was true, but it was also true of all adolescents. But as he had come to hate everything in this country, he would always say, whatever he didn't like, that it was "the influence of this country."

In addition, I was having academic problems. Before that, I had always wanted to be a doctor, and had wanted to succeed, but now I began to feel like a total failure. I rebelled desperately against my father's desire for me to succeed—and I justified it by what I felt was his failure. I started cutting classes relentlessly. But it wasn't only because of my problems at home. It was the system and being Puerto Rican.

The teachers were terribly prejudiced and they didn't try to hide the fact—actually I don't think they were even aware of it the way we would be today. But they used to say things to us that you wouldn't say as a joke today. They'd say things to us like: "You people are lazy." Or I remember one teacher saying, "Giving you an education is like throwing pearls before swine." And of course there was their resentment about money: "We work hard so our tax money can go to support you." But the thing you'd hear the most often was "You're stupid," and "You won't make it."

After a while I began to believe that. I had always been a good student before I started cutting, although I had never been and am still not good in math. They gave me a group I.Q. test and I panicked. I became blocked and frightened and discouraged and didn't answer a single math question. And of course realizing the effect this would have on my score made me worry about the other sections, so I couldn't think and answer the other questions. My score on the I.Q. test turned out to be a 73, which is technically classified as a low-grade moron. At first they didn't tell me, although I knew I had done badly, but then they shattered me by showing me my score. They did it to discourage me from taking a regular school program since they wanted me to take one of those combined work-study programs. They also assured me that I could never make it to college.

Part of it, I suppose, was sincere. They were unaware of the fact that I.Q. tests are devised by whites for whites and have a strong built-in bias against minority groups or poor people. For example, the Stanford Binet test will show you a picture of an ocean liner and ask you what's missing in the picture. The answer is a smokestack, which many rich kids who have seen ocean liners would know. But what child living in a ghetto area would have seen an ocean liner? We couldn't even afford toy boats in our bathtubs which rich children often have. There are all kinds of things like that, besides the obvious language problem. If you don't understand the question, how can you answer it?

But they also had a selfish reason for discouraging me. They resented the fact that my family and other Puerto Rican families were on welfare, and they wanted to convince me to leave school as soon as possible and support my family so they wouldn't have to. So they told me that with an I.Q. like mine, I should quit school as soon as I turned sixteen and go to work so my parents could go off welfare.

Well, I became really depressed. I went into an even deeper funk and constantly cut classes and was fresh to the teachers—all things that were really not like me. They finally referred me to the Bureau of Child Guidance. I would never have gone there in a million years had I realized exactly what it was for. They had asked me if I was unhappy and I admitted I was, because of my father, and they told me to go there and discuss my father. So I went thinking it was to help him. I didn't know that the woman was a therapist, and her job was to help me, or I would have run like hell. Afterwards I was referred to a social worker and went to her for three years, still not knowing that I was the one getting therapy. But she helped me. I did finish high school at an early age—sixteen—with an academic diploma.

Then I went to work in a factory for four years which is all they had told me that I could do. For six months I did try to go to college at night, but I still believed, as they had told me, that I wasn't college material. And I became depressed and didn't take any of my final exams. Perhaps I was afraid they were right about me. I got all "incompletes," which was the equivalent of failure. So I continued to work in factories. One was a pencil factory and I made $24 a week and got blisters on my hand from the machine. Then I worked in a book bindery collating papers at $32 a week, which, as you can imagine, was not the world's most exciting work. Afterwards I worked with radium and got more money, but that's because it was dangerous to your health. In fact every month I had to have a physical examination to make sure I could continue working there, and although the results were never good, I continued on nonetheless because of the money.

I had always like photography and so during this time, when I had a little more money, I went to a photography school at night, and later I worked in a camera shop for six days a week. Eventually I did the buying for them, and after a while worked my way up to the manager of a large chain of camera stores.

Life at home didn't improve during all this but I learned how to adjust after therapy. My stepmother became very ill from an abnormality in her blood vessels, which became serious as she grew older. In addition, she was an extreme diabetic so she began to go in and out of hospitals all the time. My father had never regained his health after his first heart attack and had in fact gotten worse. He had another major heart attack and his physical situation was complicated by lung trouble. But someone had to work once my mother got sick, so he did. He still had psychiatric problems—he never got over his depression—but he could function on a simple level. He had become a very bitter man but he still tried to hold fast to his values. He got a job as an elevator operator at a large hotel and despised every minute of it. Not only was it physically difficult for him to work, psychologically it was demeaning to him, especially since he had once been so sucessful. He finally became critically ill with heart trouble, and four months ago he died.

But before this happened, I decided to try college again. I'm sure I still unconsciously had that old sense of worthlessness but somehow I felt that this time I could make it. But when I wrote to the college, at first they wouldn't take me because I had not completed my finals that other time. Eventually they said I could try it on a six month basis. I graduated magna cum laude and Phi Beta Kappa after going to school at night. I have an excellent job now as a social worker; going to school at night I'm completing my master's degree which I should get shortly. After that, maybe a doctorate. Pretty good for someone with a 73 I.Q., eh?

THE REFORMED JUNKIE

My NAME IS JUAN. I was born in Puerto Rico but I came to America when I was two and I don't remember anything about Puerto Rico. I've got a younger brother and two older brothers so there are four kids in the family. My parents split when I was four years old. My father became a janitor and my mother ran a sewing machine and used to make clothes for people until she just couldn't keep up the speed. He was always drinking and he liked to fuck anything he could, so both of these things caused fights, since she didn't like that. Besides which, he used to beat on her whenever he could whether he was drunk or not. He just liked to hit her.

My father and I ain't never been close but I used to go to him sometimes when I needed money. I'd ask him for a dollar or two and he didn't care, but I'd go out and use it to buy a reefer. It was easy to get money from him because I would just play on his motherfucking guilt. He had plenty of that the way he treated my mother and didn't take care of his kids. I felt close to my mother and liked her, but she always had to go to work and had to leave me with different people so I never got to know her real well. I guess her leaving me with different people made me feel she wasn't giving me love, and like any kid I needed it.

School was a drag. I didn't like the old gray-haired strict white teachers that they had. You'd think in a Puerto Rican school, they might have some Puerto Rican teachers, but they never did. Just the bitchy white ones who didn't like us Puerto Ricans very much. Well they liked us if we did well. If you got straight A's, they'd give you plenty of love and attention, but if you weren't a straight A student, forget it. I wasn't an A student.

I didn't get along none too well with the teachers either. One teacher slammed a door on my arm on purpose. She was trying to break it, I think. She had it in for me because I got turned off school at an early age and wouldn't play their game. When I had nothing better to do I used to throw rocks at the windows. That was fun. One day a student brought a parakeet into school and I opened up the cage door and let him fly out. The whole class spent a lot of time trying to catch him. Then too, I did other things they didn't like. I used to toss paper clips at people a lot. I'd put gum on their seats, so when they sat down and tried to get up, they couldn't. It was a gas. But then one of the teachers tried to hit me. She told me to put out my hands so she could hit it with a ruler and I was damned if I was going to do something that stupid. So instead of sticking my hand out I just looked her straight in the eye and said, "Fuck you ma'am." And then I ran like hell.

I came back to school six months later. It wasn't that

I wanted to, but like my mother made me come back. She married this new man and she became a real drag. So was he. He was a white-American oriented Puerto Rican. They're the worst kind. He was always drinking, and he used to come home drunk and start pounding on the door for her to let him in. But she wanted no part of him when he was drunk, so he would sleep outside the door those nights. We were living in a basement then, and she had two kids by him. He always played favorites and liked them better than me. He and my mother split after six years and I was glad.

Anyway, they kept me in the ninth grade for three years and then they kicked me out. I cut school so much that they wanted to send me away, but they couldn't find me because we were always moving to a different place. And so I never went to school. Instead, I would go to parties with wine and reefers and a bunch of girls, and I used to grind up against the girls. That's when you get real close and rub up. You didn't do much else then, but I sure as hell do a lot more now. But I was younger then. There were lots of parties going on in daytime, when I was supposed to be in school. We'd all meet outside or near the school and find out whose mother was away, because that meant their house was empty for the day and we could use it to throw a party. Some of the mothers were away 'cause they worked, but then you used to get these women who were out because their husbands had died four days earlier, so they were out dancing.

So after three years in the ninth grade, I cut out altogether. I had to make some money, so what I did was start selling ounces of heroin. I didn't actually sell them, you see. I was a runner making $250 a week. Someone would order it from this other cat, and then he would send me to deliver it. I used to deliver to some of the best places, man—Park Avenue, Rockefeller Plaza. You wouldn't believe who was on drugs.

Well, I was making really good money and had enough bread for everything I wanted. Life was good. But then some stoolie told the pigs about me and when I walked out of a place carrying smack to the next place, the lousy pigs jumped me. But it was my first offense so I got probation for three years. They didn't send me up. But things got bad after that. About six months later my older brother came out of reform school. Until then I had only been blowing smoke, and he popped some gas on me and we snorted together. Actually I had tried stronger stuff than reefers before then, but it was only coke.

In the beginning I only snorted with my brother, but then I started shooting up and was getting sort of strung out. It was hard on me to get to see the parole officer each week, and I began to worry because I was always high and knew he might notice it. I had plenty of money from running, so I went to the parole officer and offered him a thousand dollars to get me off parole. Sure enough, he wrote up a report saying I'd been working and was clean, and the judge believed it and he cut me loose.

But then I got really strung out. I didn't have to show up there and look good for anybody so I spent days high. One day the dealer I was running for forgot something in my house and came back and caught me shooting up. He cut me loose because he didn't want any addicts working for him, and he stripped me of my rank. But he left me with three ounces of heroin, so I got some cats together who I knew were shooting dope and put the stuff in $5 bags and gave them $2 a bag to deliver for me. Then they ran for me, and I could sit back and take in the money. It wasn't long before I was making $400 a day from having them run for me, but me and my brother was using about $300 a day of stuff on our own. I was taking about 1/16 of an ounce a day.

I knew this cop in the neighborhood and he started to notice that I was changing. My clothes were getting funky and I was obviously strung out. So he approached and asked me what was happening. I didn't have to tell him because he knew, and he recommended that I go to a hospital. It was an experimental hospital and it was hard to get in to, but he helped me get into it. But I didn't like the place because I really wanted to get helped there and I couldn't. You see, there were about 125 guys there and maybe 40 chicks. The guys would get the girls to sell pussy to the hospital workers, and then they'd give the bread to the guys. Then the guys would use this money to buy drugs, so there were more drugs in the hospital than there were on the streets. Junkies used to call the place "paradise," and they'd put themselves in there so they could get drugs easy. It was on an island, so the guys who bought the drugs would have to swim off to get them. That was the bad part though because some drowned and some got busted on the other side. But most came back with more drugs for us.

I didn't like the place for other reasons too. It was a drag. It was a real cold place. We had three meals a day and recreation, like pool, but it was a drag, man. I wanted to get helped, but I got involved in all that shit and they had psychiatrists and psychologists and all that jazz. I really just wanted to get out. So I told them a sad sad story about my Mommy and Daddy and how I had to go home to help them. I acted serious and carried books around like I was really studying and trying and it wasn't working. I talked to them about how hostile the environment was for little old me. So I got out in four months.

Then I went to hairdressing school. What a drag, especially with all those fags around. I was always trying to screw the girls. When we were in training, I would just leave women under the driers and let their hair burn while I went around looking for a joint. They kicked me out, man. I just don't think they liked a straight hairdresser.

I've been screwing since I was eight. I had this cousin who was twelve years old and she used to babysit for me. It was a nice arrangement. She told me one day that she wanted to play house. I told her to "go fuck," which, it turned out, was what she wanted to do. She told me that to play house we had to make believe we were mother and father and take our clothes off and get into bed. I did and she grabbed my dick. I was like young, man, and didn't really know what was happening and I was too afraid to really enjoy it. I mean I liked it, but not like now. So I played house with her for a year and a half. Then I started running around with lots of girls from the neighborhoood. By the time I was fourteen, I used to chase and screw everything in skirts. But from when I was eleven until I was about fifteen I'd also go with faggots, because it was an easy way to make ten bucks. They would just bend over and that was it. But then this guy tried to fuck *me,* so I hit him on the head with a bottle. After that I didn't want nothing to do with fags no more.

At about fifteen I started pimping. Girls liked me because I was hustling drugs and making money, and girls like business guys. So then they made money for me and I didn't have to do anything for it except sometimes screw them. I fell in love at sixteen with a Puerto Rican-Chinese girl but I couldn't deal with heavy love so she cut me loose. You know, she only wanted me to see her. In the last three years I've loved two women but I'm not like some of these guys who want their wives to be a virgin. I don't want to have to teach nobody. She better know. I think a woman is important in helping a man find fulfillment. I know a girl helped me to get my act together when I was fucked up. They play a happy role. It's much deeper than screwing. But some of these girls, the old bullshit from the old country is too strong in them. They want to be dominant and possessive, so we have to beat on them a little when they get that way. It ain't good.

Well, after I dropped out of hairdressing school I really started shooting dope a lot. I also went to a lot of hospitals to get help. Some junkies go to hospitals so they can go off it and need less to get high again. It's cheaper that way because their habit costs less and it's a better high at first. They don't really want to be helped. I wanted to be helped but I wasn't. I tried every hospital in the city, and I went to one hospital six times. But I didn't go off drugs. I was so high once I went through a window. And once I was talking to a psychiatrist and dropped my cigarette and began looking for it on the floor. And I was so high that I grabbed his leg and picked that up—I didn't know the difference between a leg and a cigarette. That's how high I was. Well, I guess they all thought I really didn't want to be helped, and so they all recommended that I leave. That means they kicked me out. So I spent the next three years on drugs, and to make the money I sold them and had people running for me. But then my connection got busted and I had to do something else to get the money and started burglarizing houses.

I'd go to a house, see, and check the building. Then I'd ring a bell. If there was no answer I knew the place was empty. If someone did answer I'd say I had the wrong apartment and I'd split to another building. I didn't want anyone getting suspicious. But if it was empty, first I'd try to pick the lock, and if that didn't work I'd try to get in through the window. I'd put tape on the window so the glass wouldn't fall when I broke it. Once I got into a house I'd look for jewelry and money. Things like TV sets and radios were not my first choice. Everybody specializes, you know. Some go for credit cards, some for TVs. Me, I liked jewelry and money.

People had the damndest places to hide things. They often stuffed money in the most obvious place between the mattresses. That was always the first place to look. A lot of people hid it under the carpet. You wouldn't believe how many people put money and jewelry in books or fake books and think they're hiding it. But the funny thing is they never hide it in a Bible. You never had to look at that book. Somehow they're afraid of it. You don't find nobody who cut out the pages of a Bible to make a hiding place. I guess they're afraid God might do something to them for it. Jews often keep their money in china closets and with the silverware. If you saw by the name on the door that they were Jewish, that was the first place to look for. I often found pot stashed in refrigerators

and I'd take that too. It was sort of funny, them hiding
hash from the pigs and me finding it and stealing it. Another place they used to hide things was in the electrical
outlets. They would unscrew the outlet and there's some
space back there and they'd put an expensive ring or
something in it. But most people don't even bother hiding
things. You go to their drawers and there's their money
and jewelry. It's pretty easy to get to.

I had some close calls. Sometimes I would be working in an apartment and the owner of the place would
come in and I'd have to hide quickly. They might walk
around and not know I was there. Nobody ever did anything interesting. But I was plenty scared. Once I was
burglarizing a house and I heard the key in the door and
man, I panicked. I jumped in the closet and in came the
person and took off his coat and put it in the other closet,
and he walked around and then just sort of settled down
for the evening. I was in the closet sweating and per-
spiring and my heart would start beating fast everytime I
heard him get up, because like I thought he might find
me at any moment. Meanwhile I hadn't had a fix all day
and I wanted it something awful. I felt sick and panicked
and I had to stay in that closet all afternoon and evening
until the next day when he left again. I was really scared.

And then I got caught. I was once burglarizing a
house and was trying to open a safe and this man who
lived there suddenly comes in. And like the minute I
looked at his face I knew that man was a cop. He pulled
a pistol and I made a dive for the window. He shot me
and missed. I tried to get out of the window but he caught
me. But before he arrested me he took me to the basement of his house and cuffed me bad. He really kicked my

ass. At one point he hit me and my eye hit the corner of the wall and my face cracked open there. I've still got stitches. When I was out, he called in another blue coat and had me taken in. I got Article 9 then—that's when you get three months in the nuthouse and nine months on probation. The reason I didn't get worse and got a break was because the pig had beaten me up and the judge could see it and gave me a light sentence.

The nut house was a real drag. Just a bunch of crazy people sitting there all day and watching TV. There was nothing you could do. If you tried to shoot dope they'd send you to jail for the whole sentence. If you tried to leave, they'd send you to jail. If you sneezed, they'd send you to jail. It was a drag.

I got out and started shooting dope again and I stuck up some big pusher three weeks later. Next thing I found out that they'd put a contract on me—you know, paid someone to kill me—so I had to get the fuck out of town fast. I didn't know where to go, but I hadn't seen my father in many years and he was remarried and living in some la-de-da place. So I took a train to see him. You know how on those [commuter] trains they put their valises up top? Well before I got off the train, I took a valise I saw that was next to my coat. When I opened it, I saw that it had about 20 different credit cards. So I took the valise to my father's house and left it there, and I went downtown to see where I could score. I saw some guy rubbing his nose and knew that he was high. People on H often do things like that, or they scratch themselves. You can always tell. So I asked him where I could get some stuff and I found out, but first I had to get some money. So I burglarized a house. Then I bought some dope and some pills and took some of that, and while I was walking toward the train back to my father's house I saw a big set of drums in the back seat of a car. Now I always wanted me a drum set and thought it would be a nice thing to bring back home, so I opened the car through the side window and stole it.

The only problem was getting it home. I couldn't carry it on the train because it was too big. I couldn't even walk to the station with it. So I waited for a while until a cops car came by, and then I told them my sob story. I told them my car had broken down and that I lived with my father in —— and that I had no way to get home and I was stranded. And they gave me a ride right to my father's house.

But then my luck ran out again. I had gotten all this dope with the money from the burglary and that night I took an overdose. My father found me and he also went through the valise and found those credit cards I had stolen. He called the fuzz, and they asked me how I had gotten to my father's house. "Oh," I told them. "Some cops gave me a ride." They didn't have a sense of humor because they sure as hell didn't laugh.

I gave the judge a sad story. It was so sad that even the stenographer cried, and I made a big thing about how I wanted to go straight in life, but no one would let me. I told him how everything had always worked against me. I told him how hard it was to be raised in a city which played a big part in breaking up my parents' marriage. I told him how hard it was to live in a cold water flat where your entertainment was looking at the cracks in the walls and ceilings, or watching the cockroaches and having the rats stay up with you to watch the late late show. I talked of how school teaches us nothing relevant and how it's totally unrelated to the problems of Puerto Ricans. I told how they don't care about you if you speak Spanish and don't understand them, and how they teach nothing of Puerto Rican history to make us proud. I told him how bad schools had turned me off. I told him about the bad neighborhoods with the dope all around, and the gangs, the dealers, the prostitutes, the winos. I told him I had no choice but to lead a life of dope because it was right there, and I told him how all the hospitals I tried made me shoot more dope, and then how I was sent to jails that punished me for what was society's fault.

We're a close knitted people you know and we're broken up in New York where they don't offer you nothing. In Puerto Rico everything that's theirs is yours, and if you come into somebody's house there is nothing they won't give you. They'll share everything with you. But here they won't give you a motherfucking plate of food. You come into their house and they hide it from you. That's what New York has done to us. We're like the Jews were in Germany—fucked up, exploited, made into puppets, and only helped in token amounts. And it ain't enough.

When I was finished with that I wasn't sent to jail. I was sent to Synanon for 18 months and I stayed clean. I came back in 1965 and decided to live with my uncle because I just didn't want to go back and live with my mother, and I couldn't live with my father. But I had some problems. I screwed my uncle's sister-in-law and she got pregnant. I had tried to be cool with her because she was family and all, but she was always playing up to me and after three months I couldn't stand it and screwed her. So my uncle kicked me out of the house. I really liked her too. I had been clean for two years, but that made me very very sad. So I started again that day and I was busted again and sent to jail for seven months. I had tried to make things all right in the family by marrying her, but she got an annulment and wrote me that in jail. It was the only time she ever wrote me, although I waited the whole seven months to hear from her.

When I got out I went to see my kid but it was a bad scene. Some people had told her that I was going to steal my kid, which I wasn't, so I had to leave. I was really down again that day, what with not seeing my own kid. So I started taking drugs again. I got busted again, and that time got five years in State prison. I stayed there for two-and-a-half years. It was like a human zoo. I was caged-in about eighteen hours a day, and allowed a couple of hours in the fucking yard with nothing to do there. And the pigs were always trying to fuck you up no matter what you did. It was a real bummer.

While I was in jail I took the High School Equivalency exam and I cheated. There was a Cuban sitting next to me and he would write out the answers for me and drop them on the floor. They didn't see what I was doing, because I'd put my foot on the paper and then push it over near me. I passed the exam. And then I got a scholarship to college and did real well. I got straight A's and never went to class. I spent most of my time in college putting together a drug program to help other people with my problems. When I came out, the parole got on my ass for starting the drug program—it was political, they said. They wanted to pull me back in, but I jumped out of a second story window and went right to California, where I began doing drug counseling with Mexicans. Then I came back, and now I'm here working on a drug program for a church. I haven't used drugs in two years. Ah, that's a lie. I've gotten high about ten times in the last two years, but I'm not hooked and never will be again. Now I understand drugs and know what it can do to you so I'm going to stay clean.

THE TRUANT

My name is Miguel. I guess being a Puerto Rican is just like being anybody else, for me. It don't bother me being a Puerto Rican. Anyway, I like being a Puerto Rican. I know a lot of my friends are Puerto Ricans. I'm proud of myself and being Puerto Rican, ever since I can remember. I don't know where my father is now. He left when I was about five years old. I don't remember him, but my mother shows me pictures so I know what he looks like. He looked like me. He left because there was a big fight in the family. My mother tells me there were a lot of problems in the family, a lot of fights and arguments. He used to beat her. He would drink. And then one day he just left. Now we live off welfare. Every two weeks we get about $130 or something, for the five of us.

But we got lots of nice stuff in the apartment. When I was small, a motorcycle ran me over and we had money from that accident. And my mother used that to buy furniture and a television. I don't watch it much. I like to go out a lot, and go to movies a lot, and my mother gives me the money or I hustle it or I bum it off people I know, like my best friend. I met him when I was in the Boy Scouts a few years ago. I quit the Boy Scouts because they used to goof on me. They used to call me "stink bomb." I was dirty when I was small. I was really dirty. You know how little kids are. They don't care how they look or anything. I'd come in ripped pants and stuff, and they'd goof on me a lot. I was the guy they used to pick on, like a clown. Even my best friend used to pick on me. He'd say, "Stink bomb, get on line." In the beginning this bothered me. After a while I decided to quit. My cousin, he stayed. I heard he got mad and went after a guy with an ax, or a rake or something. His old lady would tell him to do something and he would do it. He had pride but he did crazy things. Like he shot a rock at her.

I used to like to go camping. You feel more free. You know, you walk around at night and you don't expect much to happen. Here you walk around at night and you got to watch out or you'll get jumped. I never got jumped. At least, when I was younger I got jumped. Somebody took me off for a leather I had. I was in the park with my cousin playing handball, and my cousin walked away to talk to his friend. Then there was this guy with a switch blade. He came switching it and jabbing it at me. I figured he had something against me. And this guy with the blade said, "Hey, give up the leather." And I said, "No." It was a brand new leather—a new coat, persian lamb. So I called for my cousin and he came, but one guy had a knife at my neck and another guy had a knife and he cut my hand. So my cousin said, "Give it up." So I gave it to him. The coat cost my mother about sixty dollars. And I felt real bad because my mother spent the money on me. My mother, she didn't care so much—she just said I should have given it to him without no fight.

And I got in trouble with the law, too. Sneaking in trains, riding on the rails. One time I got hit by a cop. I was writing on a wall in a station, and I was on probation at that time because I wasn't going to school. I figured, Wow, if I get caught while I'm on probation they'll try to send me upstate. Upstate is where they keep all the bad kids. It's where they lock them up. I've never been there, but I was scared so I tried to make a run for it. So I made believe I was taking out my wallet to give the policeman something to show him who I was. And then I ran. So he grabbed my jacket and pushed me down, and he got mad. He punched me, bop, right in the face, and then in the arm. He pushed me up against the fence and he said, "I had enough out of you. I want to see your identification."

When that cop hit me I got mad. I wanted to hit him back. But I didn't. He took me to an old token booth and he took my name and then he told me to take the train and leave. He said, "Go!" I didn't tell my mother but she'll probably receive a letter about it someday.

I don't like cops because I think most of them are prejudiced—they're just prejudiced. They think you're always up to something. Like one time, where I go to school now, some of us were just walking around, and a cop was called by these people because they thought we were going to do something. So the cops come and they say, "Get out of here, we don't want you around here." Two white cops, and we weren't doing anything. But I guess because we're Puerto Rican, they don't want us around. They don't call us names, but they give us dirty looks. Like, *be cool before I lock you up.*

There are Puerto Rican cops, and like one time I got caught in the train station by a Negro cop and he said, "Just ask next time, because if you don't have the money to get home and you've got to go from Manhattan to the Bronx," he said, "just ask." Then he let me go.

When you need them cops are never around. I never see a cop doing anything wrong, except the cop who hit me. I don't know why he did. He'd grabbed me already; I don't know why he had to throw a punch at me. The Negro cop, he was good, he let me slide. And I've got a lot of Negro friends. Puerto Ricans and blacks, they get along.

I got problems in school because I cut out a lot. Like when I was in the sixth grade and my friend Pedro told me to cut out for the first time, I was scared. But I liked it, so I cut out again and again, and I started getting into the habit. When I went to Junior High School I got more and more friends and I just liked to cut out of school with girls for gigs. And now that I go to school, wow, I just can't get used to it. I'm in the ninth grade and it's boring, boring. I can't wait to get out of school.

My favorite subject is gym. And my least favorite is science. If it wasn't for school I wouldn't be in trouble. That's the main problem. Like school is the main problem for everything for me. Once I go to school, things start happening. My mother starts arguing with me—if I didn't go to school I wouldn't have no problems at all. But I don't want to quit. I really don't know what I want. I just don't know what I want to be or where I want to go.

I got caught truant. The probation officer calls my mother and talks to her and they say they want to send me upstate to be locked up in jail. Some people told me about that. They say it's all right if you're cool and don't fight back. But some places, they like have homosexuals, you know, and you've got to fight. They told me they don't give you no food up there. And you have to fight for every little thing. And they all got one T.V. and you can't see what you want. You're locked up and you can't see no girls. And for me that's bad cause I'm a girl lover.

I love girls. Everybody knows that I love girls and I can't stand to be without girls. To me they're everything. Without a girl, I don't think I'd be anything. I like girls a lot. I don't know why. When I was a very young kid I wasn't interested in girls so much. But I've liked the girls since I was six years old. When I was six years old the girls used to play mommy and poppy. My next door neighbor used to come over and we used to play father and mother. We used to sleep with each other. Things like that.

When I hit Junior High School I went out the first time with girls and I really got interested in girls. That's when I really started getting together with girls. Going out with a girl for a month is the most it's ever lasted. Her name was ———. She was pretty dry. She had long hair, nice figure, you know. She was cute looking too. We didn't really go out on dates. She was in my brother's class. And I went over to him and said, "Hey, you know, I'd really like to get to know her." One day, he brought her into the lunchroom and we started talking, and I liked

her and she liked me. I asked her out about a week later
and she said "yes." We didn't go nowhere. I used to walk
her home. Asking her out was sort of like saying, "Be my
girl." And that means when you have a girl, she's yours.
She ain't nobody else's. She knows she's yours. Like you
own her, almost.

I discovered sex when I was six. There was this girl
upstairs, and she used to like sex, I guess. She used to
come down and say, "Come on," and she would give me a
quarter. Whatever she told me to do I'd do. She wanted
me, you know, to sleep with her. She'd say, "Do this,"
"Touch this." And I remember that, too. That's one thing
I'll never forget. She used to give me money and lollipops.
She was a big girl. She was about sixteen, and I was only
six. She wanted me to sleep with her and do things to
her. I used to be scared to do it. But I didn't get no feeling.
She got feeling though.

Now it's a little harder to get sex. When you get
older, it gets harder to get what you want, I don't know.
I think it's because girls get more mature and they get
scared of getting a kid. You know, when you get to be
thirteen, they develop things and you can give them a
kid. And girls get scared of that. And they say they like to
be virgins and stuff. But you always manage to get it
somehow—if you want it you can get it.

The first time I really enjoyed sex was when I was
twelve. Before that it was nothing—it was like a game, and
I didn't know what it was all about. Then I started enjoying it. At my momma's house they never talked about
it at all, but at my cousin's house they started talking
about fags when I hit thirteen. And my aunt used to talk

about sleeping around. She used to talk to me and my cousin. She'd tell us, "Be careful. Girls got diseases and stuff." You know when you hit thirteen you really start getting down to business and stuff.

I knew a guy who used to be a drug addict. He's eighteen. He's my father's brother. He used to mainline. He used all drugs. One time he got locked up, and he went away, but then he came back, and he started using drugs again. I used to cop them for him—I used to buy them for him from a pusher. It was just hard finding a pusher with good stuff. I used to go all over Spanish Harlem—wow, you can't find a good pusher any place. You'd see all your friends and ask them, and they'd tell you, "Well that guy over there can get you fixed up." So you'd ask him, and you'd get places. A bag costs $2.00. My friend earned a little money for a while. Then he started selling clothes. Forget it. But now he doesn't use drugs any more. He got religious and ain't been hooked since a month or two ago. I don't know what they call it— a church down on West 111th Street. But he's going to join the Marines.

He used drugs, but I smoked. When you smoke you feel good. You feel happy. You feel funny. You feel different. You feel like you're in the sky. You see things differently. You see them twice. I was afraid to really get hooked, so I kept off it for a long time. But my friends sometimes say, "Hey, you want some?"

One of my favorite things is getting high on liquor, but I really like getting high on coke. I like it a lot. To me it is better than being with a girl. I like sometimes, like Puerto Rican day, when we have feasts. We have meat pie, it's really good. It's stuffed with meat and then they boil it in water. That and pig. I like pig—fried or roast pig.

When I was in clicks* I seen violence and rumbles. When I was young in Junior High School there used to be a click called Thunderbirds. In the Bronx where I live now, we'd all get together and we'd have our own club in the basement. There used to be a lot of guys, and sometimes we'd get into trouble. We'd have fights with other gangs. They'd come around our block, we'd tell them to get out, and we'd start calling them names and then fight with everything we had. Sometimes it was a clean fight—one guy from one click and one guy from another click. But most of the time they used to all want to fight.

We'd go to the park and we used to rumble. We used to have chains and some guys would have bats. Sometimes I was in on it. When you rumble you really don't care—you just get wild. You don't know what you're doing. Afterwards it's fun, when you make it out alive. Sometimes you get hurt; once I got hit over my eyebrow and it took three stitches. Sometimes they lashed me with chains. One time they stabbed me in the leg, but I didn't even feel it. I didn't tell my mother nothing, and it got swollen. I still got the mark. And I got cut around with my face. There's scars now. The worst thing that ever happened was one of the boys cracked his head real bad and he was in the hospital. I don't know what really happened to him. That was the worst.

What's bad about being Puerto Rican up here is most of us become junkies—they don't get jobs, they

* Probably from "cliques."

don't get a thing. They don't get fair treatment, the same as other people—like whites. They don't get famous. You hardly meet any famous Puerto Ricans. When I was smaller I had comic book heroes, like Spider Man.

People ought to know that Puerto Ricans are not so bad as people think. Most whiteys think they are wild criminals. They think Puerto Ricans are going to want to kill you or something. And, like, white girls are so conceited. You try to talk to a white girl, you say, "Hello there, baby," and she says, "Why don't you drop dead," or something. Almost anyplace. Most of them are like that. Like white men. Sometimes they get loud with you. Like when I get in a train I can't stand it when I try to go out, and I say, "Excuse me," and then they push you, and they say, "Why don't you watch where you're going?" They push you and won't let you out. They get like that with me, and I get like that with them. One time a guy wanted to fight with me cause the door locked.

White people, they like to get fast with you. They like to pick on you. They take advantage. . . . Most Puerto Ricans agree, they're rotten. If I had a lot of white people in front of me, I'd cuss them out. I don't know what I'd say, but I'd cuss them out—I'd think of something rotten to say.

THE FIGHTER

MY NAME IS RODRIGUES. In 1950 I came over from Puerto Rico. I was almost two years old then. My mother took me here because she had left my father. The marriage had been a very bad one. He was almost thirty years older than she was and I don't know why she even married him except it may have had something to do with defying my grandmother who had told her not to. Besides which he was wealthy and had his own business, so I guess she thought marriage would give her a chance to live the type of life she would never have been able to know. But it was doomed to failure, mostly because she was only sixteen years old at that time, which is kind of young anyway. Here she was a young woman and she was kind of wild and wanted to go out all the time and be free. And all he wanted to do was take care of the business and work all the time. But she was young and wanted something of life. Furthermore, he had a lot of responsibilities because he had been married before and had 12 young children by that marriage who are now my stepbrothers and sister.

One of the boys was older than my mother when she became his stepmother. So their marriage lasted only a year and then my mother took me to New York to start again.

I lived with my mother and she worked in a factory. She made about $42 a week. We were also living with my grandmother, some cousins and my uncle, so it was pretty crowded with seven of us living there in just three rooms. There was a kitchen-dining room and two bedrooms. Actually there had been a living room but we had to make it into a bedroom so there was no place to entertain. If we wanted to have fun, my cousin would take us out and we would play in the street.

Soon after we came to New York my mother remarried—an Arabian salesman. The marriage was new, and I guess she felt it would work better if there were no children around so she left me to live with my grandmother. I liked living with her because I was her favorite. Furthermore, she made money by babysitting for my aunts and friends of the family, so when they went to work, they brought all the children over to her and she took care of all of us. She didn't charge much; I don't think she made more than two or three dollars a day for the babysitting and she didn't collect welfare, so financially we weren't too comfortable. This lasted until I was about six years old.

School was a real hassle. There were only about ten Puerto Rican children in the school at that time and I used to get beat up every single day on my way home. It never failed. There was no reason to beat me up—just that I was Puerto Rican and different. My grandmother used to worry about it more than me because she became afraid that I would seek the wrong kind of friends—you know, join a gang of tough boys—to protect myself. God, I remember one incident quite vividly. Two classmates, they were brothers, told me one day that they were going to beat me up. When I left school that afternoon there were three of them waiting outside. One of them held me down and the other two just kept hitting me. I told the principal, but he wouldn't do anything about it. Maybe he was afraid of what they'd do, or what their parents would do, or maybe he was too busy. Or maybe he just didn't care if another Puerto Rican got beat up. I don't know, but it continued like this until I was about in the fifth grade.

My grandmother didn't have to really be afraid, because there were no gangs that would take a Puerto Rican at that time, so I had no gang to join. So I was smart and I started my own. I guess it's what you'd call a gang, but I called it a club then. I called it: "The Young Puerto Ricans," and by that time there were more of us around so I got them all to join it for protection. There must have been about fifty kids, if you count those from the elementary school along with those in the junior high. The purpose was to protect ourselves, but also to get back at the others who had always beaten us up. I suppose it really started solely for protection, but some of the kids wouldn't use it just for that, and since we were a large group, and pretty tough, they'd go out looking for a fight. Most of the kids we fought were white. Some of our kids were a little more smarter than just to attack them. They would instigate the fight so that the other group would start it—you know, they'd say something nasty to the white kids and then the white kids would come after them, and then they'd say, "Well I'm a Puerto Rican and he hit me first." Or it might be something subtle, like one of our group would go over to the white kids and say, "You know the air is kind of foul around here." They'd cut the white people down, but indirectly. As to who would win the fight, it was a standoff. Sometimes they would really tear us up and sometimes vice versa. I still have plenty of scars and marks from those gang fights as well as from the earlier beatings before I got protection.

I left the gang when I was in the eighth grade. I was still living with my grandmother, because my mother still wanted to live alone with that Arabian. I didn't think much of him—in fact, I couldn't stand him. He used to do things like throw me against the wall or bounce me up to see how high I would go. Actually, though I didn't know it then, he resented me bitterly because I was a boy and my mother had had three children by him and had given him only girls. So he was very bitter about it because he wanted the family name carried on. Later I saw Henry VIII on TV and it reminded me of that. My mother did have one son but he died at birth from pneumonia, which made his unhappiness even worse. It seemed that God just wouldn't give him a son. I found out years later from his brother that that was the reason he hated me. He used to tell his brother that, and that's why he despised and beat me. Later when I got older my mother wanted me to spend time with him, which I did, to make her happy. And I would sit back and analyze him as to why he would do the things he did. And I kind of understood it myself. He was too stubborn to ever apologize for the way he treated me, but I never held it against him. But that doesn't mean that I like him, or ever will. I won't.

When I was eleven and in the eighth grade, I had to

return to Puerto Rico because I got into a little bit of trouble. I took a couple of things from a relative. Actually, I don't think he was a relative but Puerto Ricans are very close, and if you're friendly with someone you'll call them a cousin or uncle. Then when your child is born, you'll introduce him as an uncle and the child grows up without distinguishing blood relatives from friend relatives. Anyway, I took five dollars from his wallet. I don't know why I did it, because I knew I'd get caught. None of us were rich enough so that the disappearance of five dollars wouldn't have been noticed. But I just wanted it and took it. Maybe I was angry because they always used to say that if you want anything like money or clothes, "Just ask and we'll give it." But I knew better—I knew that even if I had asked, they wouldn't have given it to me. Well, my uncle was very upset and tried to hit me but my grandmother wouldn't let him. Of course he kept insisting that if I had just asked he would have given it to me, which made it seem bad in my mother's eyes. But it just wasn't true. But my uncle convinced my mother that I was a hopeless thief and would end up in jail for stealing cars or something, just because of this lousy five dollars. And he seemed to think that the best way to stop me was to send me to reform school right then. Well, my grandmother wouldn't accept that, so there was sort of a compromise: I was sent away, but not to reform school—I was sent to Puerto Rico to live with my aunt.

When I first got there it was an even bigger hassle than life had been in New York. I had learned Spanish at home, and the New York kids made fun of me for speaking Spanish and not English. But by the time I got to Puerto Rico they started calling me "gringo." And that pissed me off because I had spent so much time fighting in New York, and they'd kept calling me, you know, "a lousy spic"—and now I ended up in Puerto Rico getting beat up by my own people and for being American. So I just fought back the way I had in America until they came to respect me because they saw that I didn't back away. Sure, I got my head bashed in a few times, but it wasn't only whether you won a fight that was important—it was whether or not you ran away from it. If you stayed and faced it and fought back, then win or lose you'd get respect.

But meanwhile I spent most of the school year fighting, not studying. And then I had an argument with the shop teacher, and because of that one class they told me I would lose a whole year. So I came back to New York. I lived in the same old neighborhood with the same family. I was with my grandmother again so that was O.K., and I kept my nose clean for a while. I had a few more school fights again for being a Puerto Rican, because I had to re-establish myself and show that I wouldn't take anything from nobody. And then I started cutting classes because I was getting pretty tired of school. And the dean, he was white, told me I was going to go to jail for cutting and I would have to take the whole year again unless I got an A which was nothing less than an 80% on a number of tests. I took them and the lowest grade I got on any test was 95.

I was 14 when I slept with my first girl. She lived next door to us and was older than me. I think she was about 18. I did it because the other boys defied me to. It was an experience I hadn't had and I was afraid. But she was always making advances to me and I had to prove to her and my friends that I was a man. I was more or less infatuated with her for about six months before this, and my friends had said I wouldn't dare approach that girl and I told them they were right. So they conned her into approaching me. One day she called and said she wanted me to meet her parents that night in her apartment. I believed her and fixed myself up and went there and discovered her parents weren't there. I suppose that had I been really reluctant I would have left then. But I stayed, hoping that one thing might lead to another, but I certainly wasn't going to take the first step. In fact, I wasn't sure what the first step was. I can't say I really liked it, because I was too scared to like it or not like it. She said she liked it, but I only believe half of what I hear. The affair continued on and off for a long while and then it died out.

Well, then I was in high school and I very much wanted to take computing but my grandmother wanted me to become an accountant. But although I took courses to please her, I soon lost interest because I was studying for something I didn't want to be. And I was still spending more time in fights than in the classroom. I finished that one year and then my family moved back to Puerto Rico. I took a half a year more in school there and then I dropped out and I never went back.

I stayed in Puerto Rico for a while and worked as a clerk, which I didn't like, and then as a diamond cutter, which I did like until my mother had to spoil everything because she got this irresistible urge for the first time in her life to see her beloved son, and I had to drop everything and fly back to New York. I would have liked to have stayed but I had to come back to her.

So I lived with my mother and stepfather for the first

time and hated it because he was still so cruel to me. So at the age of seventeen, right on the nose, my birthday, I joined the army so I could get away from them. I would have done anything to get out of that house.

The first few months were pretty good and kept me active, but then the next months were very bad. I wanted to go into the infantry but they said that my tests showed I'd be better in supplies, and it was just like going back to school because I had to take all these courses. So then one day they told me they were sending me to Texas to take another course, and I'd had it. I went A.W.O.L. But I had no place to go but back home, and that was worse than being in the army. I had forgotten how bad it was, and my stepfather was, and now I remembered again. So I turned myself in. They gave me a court martial and I lied like it was going out of style. I gave them a real sad story about how I was the father of a child whose mother had died at a very young age, and I had to take care of this little child and I couldn't do it in the army. And after I gave them this terribly sad story about my beloved wife dying, I hit them with another story about my current girlfriend's being pregnant and how she was about to have my other child. And because the first wife had died in childbirth, I had terrible fears that something was going to go wrong again and so I'd dropped everything to come home and take care of her so two of my children wouldn't be without a mother. Not only did they believe all that, but I actually had one of the judges crying. They gave me a suspended sentence.

Actually it was a funny story for me to choose, although it worked because I was always a little slow in sex. I guess I was too busy fighting to have much time. Now I think I would like my wife to be a virgin but it's not a requirement for marriage. I'm seeing a girl now—she's a Puerto Rican—but I'm not sleeping with her because she's a very high strung girl of strong religious beliefs. She's a Jehovah's Witness.

As for me, I don't have any religion. My grandmother was Pentacostal. They're very strict people and don't believe in smoking, drinking, going to movies, wearing makeup, or dancing. I don't think they believe in very much except for the Father, the Son and The Holy Ghost. I don't go to church. I would like to think I believe in God, but I'm not sure. I just don't know. Most Puerto Ricans are religious because of their Spanish background. But I don't consider myself like most Puerto Ricans.

Certain things disturb me about it. There are times when I read in the paper that a Puerto Rican did something bad, and it bothers me. It's not that I feel ashamed of my people, but it upsets me because I know people will see him as an example of what other Puerto Ricans are like. I would never do anything to make my people look bad, although I would fight to defend them. But I had enough fighting when I was younger. Now I try to keep my nose clean.

THE HOMING PIGEON

MY NAME IS BERNARDO. I'm twelve years old now. The first place I lived in was a rundown house, very run down. Really really bad. And I think there were five of us living there then. It was really crowded. Sometimes I had to sleep with my brothers in the same bed and we would all fight for the blanket. But it wasn't so bad as the houses across the street. Across the street, like the stairs were so bad the kids used to break their legs there just walking down the stairs. But they couldn't get them to the hospital fast because they would call the ambulance but they didn't always come. And no taxis stop here cause they always put on their off-duty lights and as they drive by they sort of smile, like hot-shit-here-I-am-and-there-you-are shit.

And then when I was five or six years old, we moved to a two-family house and I really liked it. Sometimes, before I go to sleep or when I'm in school, I like to think of being back there and having all my friends there, and we will have gold carpeting—real gold to walk on—and curtains so no one can look in. We don't have curtains now. But you could open the curtains to that house and look out at the backyard. Cause it really had a backyard, that house.

But in this backyard there used to be pigeons and my brother used to catch them with one of his friends. They put out some pigeon food to try to get them to come and eat, and then when they came over, WHAM. We'd catch them with a net and then pull down and grab them by the feet. Did they make noise. And we'd keep them in a cage for a couple of months until they became homing pigeons. At the beginning we used them for messages to each other, but it became kind of silly because my brother and me we lived in the same house and my friends all lived on the same block. So we sold them instead.

And then my brother became a drug addict for about six years. I don't know how he got hooked. I was very young at the time, but I remember we used to come from school and see the whole house messed up and we used to think somebody must have stole things. But it was just my brother trying to get money—he would tear up everything looking for it. He thought we were hiding it from him but there wasn't no money. If we had any we'd spend it.

When my brother was on drugs, my mother, she had a lot of pain. She was sick a lot. But she couldn't be in the house all the time because she had to work 'cause the welfare was never enough. She was the only one working because my other brother was in school. She packed pocketbooks or something like that. She went to a factory every day but when she came home, she used to fight with my brothers a lot. My brother, he got sent to jail a couple of times. One time he was selling something—I think it was a radio and I think he stole it. He sold it to this guy and the guy turned out to be a cop. He went to jail.

Then he got in trouble again and he was threatened, so he talked to my mother about it and they sent him to a camp where they could help him kick the habit. And he went over there and they helped him out. And he kicked it. It was amazing. He studied about life there and right now he's a minister. He's assistant director of a big place and he helps a lot of guys with the same problems he had, you know. And whether they're blacks, whites, Puerto Ricans, it doesn't really matter. I'd like to be like him— not take drugs but help people.

My other brother used to smoke marijuana, but neither of my brothers never offered me drugs. I'm glad, because I wouldn't have tried it. I'm afraid of it, because I see people walking down the streets all doped up and the way they look. And then I see pictures of narcotics addicts with their veins looking funny and things like that. I just don't want to be like that. I don't think I need that.

My brothers are tough. In a way I think it's important to be tough. But I don't think I'm tough. Like there's a lot of kids in school that push people around and stuff like that. Everyone's scared of them. But I just can't seem to be able to grab and hit a guy. I don't think I have the guts. That's what the guys say about me and they're right. I don't like it when they say it, but I know it's true. I don't think I have the guts to go over and hit someone because I'm afraid I might hurt them. If I ever have to defend myself I guess I'll do it, but I just can't stand seeing a person hurt. When I hurt a person, later on I feel bad. One time my sister she was running and I tripped her on purpose. I thought it was nothing, like it was funny, but when I got older I started thinking about it. She was about thirteen or fourteen at the time and she just hurt herself with a cracked lip. It was nothing. But I feel bad. I don't hurt nobody if I can help it.

On television sometimes they take actual pictures of people falling out of windows. I can't stand to watch. I'm afraid they may hurt themselves. I know I'm different. I know I have my own understanding of things. There's something in me that makes me that way. I think different from them. I want to do my own things.

People in the army are tough. A lot of guys go into the army and they only smoke marijuana all the time and they come back hooked on heavy drugs. Like my brother. I guess they figure the law won't do anything to them because it's legal over there. But when they come back, some of them are worse off over here than they were over there.

Most of the time I think I have it pretty good. After all, I'm Puerto Rican. Most white people don't want us to stay here and stay on welfare. They don't want us to get into a higher step—they don't want to give us money so we can. I don't know why. I have nothing against them. That's their way. I like blacks too. The only thing wrong with the black people is that they cause a lot of riots, just like Puerto Ricans. Because they're trying to go higher.

White people should give everybody else a chance. Why should they have all the money? Instead of fighting us, they should think that we're both human beings and the same thing whoever be in office, President or what.

There's never been a Puerto Rican President. If there's any famous Puerto Ricans I don't know them. I guess the only Puerto Rican hero is the guy who dis-

covered Puerto Rico. I don't know his name right now—
Ponce de Leon, I think.

If there's anything about Puerto Ricans I don't like,
it's that they talk too much. Like we're in school and the
teacher tries to calm everybody down but they keep on
talking. The Puerto Ricans. You've got to stand up and
whistle or something. Like in the train, the Puerto Ricans
speak Spanish so loud. They joke and run across the train.
I'm there sitting down and doing nothing. And I'm quiet,
but I feel the people looking at me because they see
Puerto Ricans making such a racket, and because I'm a
Puerto Rican, they think I'll do the same. I have to say
sometimes I'm ashamed to be Puerto Rican.

I also don't like being Puerto Rican because I don't
like living here. When I was a little child I could have
been killed and I wouldn't have even known it. You walk
down the street and you don't know who's in back of you
or who's in the hallway waiting for you. Terrible things
happen to people here all the time and I don't mind
admitting I'm often afraid.

Like we were robbed one time. They took our TV and
our radio. We didn't like it but what could we do? We
didn't call a cop because we didn't want to cause anything.
I just don't know why. We just don't want to get involved.
As for cops, there's plenty involved in drug stuff and viola-
tions and things like that. I've heard a lot about policemen
doing wrong things. They tell me if you pass a red light
and you give the policeman five dollars he'll let you go. I
don't have a car but that's what I heard. But when we was
robbed, my mother was sad. Real sad. We only had the
TV about a week. It was brand new. We had this other

small television but it kept jumping around a lot. Some neighbors think they saw the people who robbed it. They were Puerto Rican. Maybe they stole it because they were drug addicts and they needed money. That's what happens. It happened to my brother.

In the summertime, it's dangerous. One time I saw an accident, about three years ago when I was nine. This kid was running after a ball without looking, and this postal car hit him. And then another time my mother was with my father and this taxi hit a two- or three-year old kid who was crossing the street. And it just took the kid and ripped him around the wheels. I didn't see it but my mother saw it and she felt terrible about it. And I was real sad. I can't stand listening to things like that.

Sometimes there's violence. Last year in the summer there were about three walkouts in my school and the cops came and there was some violence. The last one was because they were going to cut out the bus passes, and the kids started arguing if they had the money to fight in Viet Nam, they should have the money to help kids with bus passes. Some kids got hurt. Real bad.

Mostly I try not to worry about things. I'm happiest in church and I want to be a minister like my brother. Our church used to be a funeral parlor but right now it looks like a church. I come back to the church when I find myself kind of lonely. I really didn't have . . . I was trying to look for something . . . I tried mostly everything. But I didn't find it. I went to church and I really put my mind into it. I really found the place where I always wanted to be.

I have a lot of sad moments. Sometimes when I'm alone and no one can see me, I cry. I had a lot of friends.

I used to like girls you know a lot. Until this year. But they didn't go for me. I used to try everything. I talked to them, tried to be nice, tried to get their attention and tried to be bright—it used to bother me a lot. I really and truly liked girls.

I guess I still do. But they don't like me. They don't *like* me. I know I'm not that handsome, but when I fix myself up I can look sharp. Once last year there was this beautiful girl. She had the most beautiful legs in the world. And I fell in love with her, and I used to wait for her after class, you know. And she was real nice to me. Like real nice. But then I found out she had a crush on my brother. . . . I guess she was just being nice to me so he would like her better.

But I don't like to talk about the past. I like to think about the future. When I'm in church I often think of heaven. That would be home for me. My greatest wish is to go to heaven because it's a beautiful place. The streets are paved with gold bricks. It's beautiful. Actually, it looks better than what I described. It's important to me. I know heaven is a nice place, and I know I'll get there one day. Because God promised me I would.

THE REFORMED THIEF

MY NAME IS CARLOS. I started stealing when I was very young because I had to take care of myself. My father— well, I call him my father because he was living with my mother then, but I don't know if he was really my father— anyway he left my mother and she would go out to work every day around seven o'clock and come back around seven o'clock at night. My older brother and my three sisters were supposed to take care of me, but they weren't going to hang around a house with a little kid so they used to take me with them. One of them is in jail now for holding up a liquor store, but in those days he didn't do anything more than just take a few things from stores. It was like a real game. He started with little things like a comb, or maybe some trading cards, but those things could really add up.

I remember one day when I was about eight we just went from store to store clipping little things—nothing over a dollar, I don't think. And by the end of the day we'd have I think it was $131 worth of stuff. I don't know what my brother did with it, because he didn't start selling stuff until he got older. But it was sort of fun. I used to help him. He would clip the item and then put it in a bag he had given me to carry. We were careful. A few times we did get caught, but he would always say that I had done it and that I was just too young to know any better. And then he would scold me there in front of the manager or detective or whoever caught us, and tell me all about how bad it was to steal. And then when we got out of the store, he'd laugh. One time I think he took a pretty big item. I was quite young then and I was carrying a box which was empty, but it had these phony sides you could just stuff things into. And he got into a big argument with the manager and he kept saying, "The kid doesn't know any better." And then all of a sudden he slapped me across the face. Real hard. Then he said something like, "that'll teach you to steal," and he pulled me out of the store.

I was crying—I didn't know what had happened. And when we got around the corner, where they couldn't see us, my brother stopped and turned to me. He said, "I'm sorry kid, but that's life."

When I got a little older he took bigger things and did it better. He used to walk into a TV or radio place and swipe a radio off the first counter and pull the price tag off. Then he'd bring it to the back counter and say something like, "My mother bought this radio here last week and she told me to bring it back to have it fixed, because it isn't working so good." And they were so stupid they would fiddle around with it and try to figure out what was wrong. And then they'd say something like, "Oh well, it's working now." And then he'd say, "Oh thanks. I'll tell my mother. Thanks a lot." And then he'd walk out with it.

It was easier to get away with this in Puerto Rican stores than in white ones, because the white people would look at a Puerto Rican kid coming in, and like they didn't trust you immediately and would keep watching you.

Another trick we used to pull was to cause them to look away so we could grab something. Like, I would knock something over, oranges, say, in a supermarket, and then the manager or somebody would run over. And then my brother would steal something from another part and run out, and I would meet him later. The louder the noise we made the more the people would run over, and then the easier it was to take something else.

Another thing we used to do was to buy one item and steal two, you understand? Because the minute you bought something they weren't suspicious. So you buy a $1 item and steal a $100 item. And I used to think it was so funny when they'd say, "Thank you" for that $1 sale. Because they didn't realize you'd just gotten them for a hundred.

After a while my brother got into trouble and he went away and I didn't steal any more for a while. I just never thought about doing it without him. You know, it had been something I had done to please him, or be with him, and it gave us something in common, and there was no reason to steal without him.

I was in school then, and I guess things were pretty good. But then I got in with this group of kids who used to go into stores and take things. Sometimes they'd all go into one store together because then there'd be so much confusion the owner wouldn't know what was happening. And the kids used to pick up all the different things, and the clerks would spend time on the kids that looked like they were buying. And it wasn't until after they left that they'd realize that maybe twenty things were gone. Well, I didn't want to go along with this at first. My brother was in trouble for stealing, and when my parents had found out they'd carried on and called him terrible names. And they kept asking him why he wasn't like me, and saying I'd never do such a thing. And my brother was kind of good to me, I guess, because he never told them he'd taken me along on these early trips. Maybe he was trying to protect me—but maybe he knew he'd have gotten it worse if they knew he had involved me. And like my parents had been proud that I hadn't been involved and I was afraid that if I ever got caught and they found out, then they wouldn't be proud of me and would think of me the way they think of my brother. So I tried to keep out of it.

But my friends used to call me names because I wouldn't go along when they stole. Like, you know, "chicken" and "sissy." And it got to be kind of hard. I wanted them to think of me the way they thought of the others. And I had special problems because we didn't really live in a Puerto Rican neighborhood and my friends were white, so it was even more important that they accept me. But then there was this conflict with my parents. Well, finally, one day we were outside of the five and dime, and they said they wanted to go in and get some candy. I knew that didn't mean they planned to go in and buy it. And I was just sort of trying to get away, like, "Oh Christ I gotta go home and do my homework now." But I guess they understood that I was trying to sneak out. And they made a big thing of it: "Coward." "Queer." "You wouldn't dare." "You don't have the guts, man." So I did it. I just went in and walked over to the candy counter and picked out a box of candy big enough for all of us. I looked around and made sure no one was looking, but there was just this stupid bunch of sales-women around. And I put it under my jacket and my heart was pounding so bad because I thought, *if I get caught man this is the end*. And then I walked out and gave it to the kids. Like they really respected me. They didn't call me chicken no more.

But that night I had a dream. I don't dream much but sometimes I do. And I remember that I was stealing something. Something big—not a box of candy. And I looked around and made sure that no one was around and I grabbed the thing—I don't even remember what it was. And as I was walking out someone suddenly put their hand on my shoulder. I turned around and I knew I had been caught. And then the funniest thing happened. I woke up suddenly and found I was pissing in my bed. I hadn't done that since I was about six. You understand, I wasn't pissing out of fright. It was like relief that I had been caught. I think I really wanted to be. And after that I never took anything from anyplace again.

THE FATHERLESS CHILD

My name is Rosita, and I'm sixteen now. When I was eight we came here. It was so different in Puerto Rico. We lived with my grandmother, grandfather, and the whole family in one great big house. It was beautiful, and we had a lot of room and a lot of flowers and a lot of trees. We came here because my uncle was living here. My mother came first and then sent for all of us. The trip here was no good at all. I didn't like it. I was vomiting and the plane was acting funny. I didn't want to leave Puerto Rico at all. I like it in Puerto Rico and wanted to stay there. I like everything—the houses, the country, and the schools. And I didn't like it here at all. I just didn't like the way it was, and I didn't understand the language so good. I also had trouble making friends because I was shy. It was different from Puerto Rico. In Puerto Rico it never snowed. It was like always having a vacation—just fun. But I like it better here now. I can go out by myself more than I could in Puerto Rico. In Puerto Rico my mother wouldn't let me go out any place by myself. I always had to go out with friends, not only because she worried about me, but because everything was so far away and you had to find someone who could take you.

When I was about six we used to have this lady who took care of me. She was sort of a nurse and she kept the house clean, because my father was in the army then, and my mother used to be away working all the time. When my father came back, I don't know what happened between them. My mother later said this lady took my father away. But when he came home he didn't seem to like her, because he never talked to her or looked at her. I used to feel badly because I liked her and he didn't. My room was next to hers downstairs, and I felt better when I heard his voice there, talking to her. And then when he left with her, I thought he must have needed someone to take care of his house and that's why he took her. And then my mother told me she was evil. But she wasn't— because she was my real mother. But he wasn't really my father. I don't know where my father lives or who he is—my real father hasn't lived with us since I was very small. So this was another father.

But about three years after they left he came back to my mother and they got married again with a real wedding. And I was so happy. I missed my nurse too, but when I told my mother that she slapped me and told me she would never be back again. But then my father went back to her. He's still with her now. I miss him very much. My father's tall and chubby. He's not a good person, my mother told me. I never really had a chance to meet him for a long time, but my mother always talked about him. I don't love him. I love my mother.

Puerto Rican families are more stricter than American families. My mother treats me different than the way my friends' mothers act toward them, although they're Puerto Rican too. My mother is real strict. When she says something, you have to do it. You can't say she's wrong or she'll hit you. But I love her very much.

I still miss my father though, especially when I have problems—most especially when I have problems with my mother. Sometimes we have arguments and if I'm alone I make believe I'm talking to my father about it. And he tells me I'm right. My mother and me fight mostly about guys. Sometimes when I go out my mother says, "Where do you think you're going?" And then she starts saying I do bad evil things in school, and that we don't behave the way we're supposed to and the way she acted when she was young. So I have my arguments with her and she gets very angry when I say I wish I were with my father. But then I think it over, and I say to myself that sometimes my mother is right. But she believes whatever people tell her about what I'm doing, and sometimes it's true. Sometimes it's not.

At first when I came here I wasn't doing good in school so my mother used to say, "You try harder cause I know you can do it." She believed in me, because in Puerto Rico I used to be one of the best students in the class. But things were different here, and they didn't speak my language. And she'd say, "Just because you came here, it's no excuse. You know the language better than that." She'd say this in Spanish and I'd understand her. But now she says, "I bet you were thinking about boys. That's all you're thinking about. That's why you don't do well in school." She used to say that all I liked was boys, but other than my first boyfriend, I only loved one other.

I had my first boyfriend when I was six years old and living in Puerto Rico. I guess I really wasn't like the way I go out today on real dates, but there was this boy I liked very much. I still remember him. He used to come to my house and sing and play the guitar. I think he was twelve. His whole family played the guitar and sang. All the Puerto Rican girls used to like him. And then one day he said he would show me something interesting and he pulled down my clothes and took his off. I ran away and told my mother he had done a real bad thing and he should be punished. But I was the one that got beat real bad. And after that I was never allowed to see him again. I don't remember his name.

The other boy I loved, his name was Juan. That wasn't his real name, but that was what they called him. I went out with him many times. My mother didn't like him at all. She would say she didn't think he liked me and he only wanted one thing, and I shouldn't give it to him.

I like guys because of the way they dress and the way they look, but I guess especially I like the way they dress. I also like the way they talk, and the way they act. It's not like girls. I like it especially when they're nice to me. I don't like nobody to boss me around. Juan tried at first to boss me around and I told him not to—I told him, "You do what *I* say." And now, when I tell him things, he usually ends up doing what I say.

I don't know about sex much because I haven't tried it yet. I don't think I'm old enough. I think before I have sex, first I have to finish school, and then my career is first. I plan to become an actress. But no boy ever asked me to have sex. Maybe if Juan did I would. But he just wants to play around—like kiss it and stuff. But he respects me. Respect depends on the way the girl acts. I like for a boy to respect me and I like to respect the boy. I don't want to be like other girls. They're too much like whores. And I don't like to be one of those whores. My mother always tells me I'm a whore. Especially if I'm late even five minutes coming home with a girlfriend. But I'm not, because I'm a virgin.

It's very important for a Puerto Rican girl to be a virgin. When she goes out with a guy, the guy's got to know how he stands. And that's important. If you get married to a Puerto Rican man the first thing he wants to know is if you're a virgin. If you're not a virgin you can forget it—it will never go. My friends tell me you can put stuff like iodine on the sheets, and that there's even an operation that makes you look like a virgin. They do it in Japan, they say. But why bother? I think every girl that plans to get married by the church should be a virgin. You just shouldn't have sex before you're married. I don't think that's right.

I like church. I pray to God a lot. I know there's a God because the Bible says there's a God. And I believe in heaven too. Of course I want to get into heaven and girls who aren't virgins when they marry don't. They go to hell. My mother told me. I think you go to heaven when you don't do nothing bad here. I don't want to go to the other place. Ever. So every night before I go to sleep, I pray. I pray for a lot of things. One time I liked this guy so much so I prayed he wouldn't be so shy and he'd just ask me out. I still like him and he's still shy. I don't know if my prayers did any good. I know he likes me. But he's so shy he never asks me.

Prayers help if you pray with your heart. I don't know what my mother prays for, but I know she makes me pray with her. She makes me do the rosary with her. And I often secretly pray that I could become a real actress. That's what I want to be. I enjoy acting a lot. I like to be somebody else once in a while. Sometimes I don't like being me. I'd like to be like Rita Moreno. I like the Spanish actresses too. The way they act, they really act real. I want to be a Spanish actress too. But if I can't become an actress, I want to take secretary courses. But I don't want to become a secretary. I like school because you learn a lot so you can get a better job. I don't want to work in a factory, like my mother had to work in the fabric factory so many years.

I know a lot of girls in my neighborhood who are on drugs, but nobody ever offered me any. You can tell the girls who are on drugs by the way they look. And they never come to school. They're taking drugs and seeing men who pay for their drugs. Sometimes I feel a little sorry for them, but I don't think they have to take drugs if they don't want to. They could just be like everybody else. Like me, for example, when I'm going to be an actress. That would make me happiest in the whole world to become an actress. Also to have a good family. And to have good times, like having no problems.

Sometimes I regret talking back to my mother. Sometimes I try not to do it but it always comes out. I can't help it. And sometimes I fight with my friends. My best friend's name is Dorita. We help each other out a lot. My mother knows her and she likes her. She's sixteen too. My family knows her and lets me sleep at her house and she sleeps at mine.

I had another friend once but we had a fight. We were real mad at each other. I was talking to this man, you see, and she thought I was talking about her mother. But I didn't say nothing about her mother. Nothing. So I got real pissed. And then she got real pissed at me. We started arguing and fighting and screaming real loud. But we didn't hit each other. When we first came here from Puerto Rico I had a fight with a girl. She was always picking on my sister. They were real tough girls, and I was plenty scared of them. But one day I was so mad I had a fight, and although that girl was much bigger than me, I won. I pulled her hair and did lots of things. I pulled her hair down below and I pinched her, and I had long nails so I scratched her face and tried to scratch her eyes. It's a good thing I didn't have no razor, because she was real tough—bossing everybody else around. But then I gave her two black eyes and now I'm the one who bosses her around. Like with Juan. I don't really like it—I mean I'm not that type, but she used to do it to my sister. Now she don't pick no more fights with me, I'll tell you.

Puerto Ricans don't have to look for trouble but if you look for trouble with them, you're sure you'll get it. Puerto Ricans don't let nobody step on them. Like one time I went to Madison Square Garden to a wrestling match. And there were these three guys sitting up in front. I was rooting for Pedro Morales but they weren't—they were for Tonoca. So every time Pedro Morales threw him to the floor, I hit these guys on the head, because I was so mad at them. And they didn't say nothing. They were just laughing. Afterwards I said to them I was sorry. But Pedro Morales won anyhow.

Puerto Ricans are loud and emotional. I'm very sentimental. If you're one of my best friends and you say something I don't like, I start crying. I cry a lot. I cry on New Year's Eve every year. I guess I cry on New Year's because I miss my father. I know it's another year that he hasn't come back and I cry because I know he won't come back next year neither. Sometimes I pray that he'll come back, especially when I argue with my mother. Sometimes when I'm praying with my mother, I'm secretly praying that my father will come back.

I fight with my mother, but me, I get along with everybody else. If they get along with me, I get along with them. When I know somebody is not going to be good, then I just don't have anything to do with them. You can tell by the way they act. Like I know in school there's some girls I don't get along with. Sometimes they're Puerto Rican.

Like people say Puerto Ricans are treated bad, and they're killed and they're poor. But these are people that live in the ghetto. I don't know because I never lived in the ghetto. Me, I've never been hungry and I've always had enough to eat. I live in a good place. But I read a lot about other places. Like I read a book about Angela Davis for a book report. And they say how the Puerto Ricans are treated bad, and are put in jail.

I think Angela Davis is trying to prove that she's innocent. I think she is. I like her. You know what she stands for in society: she's trying to help her people. She's trying to help other people too. The only people the Puerto

Ricans have like Angela Davis are the Young Lords. Sometimes I like the Young Lords, but sometimes I don't. They're trying to get more and better things for the Puerto Ricans so they can make things better. But sometimes they're too revolutionary and they fight, and I don't like fighting.

When I first came, I liked it here. But now I don't. I want to go back to Puerto Rico after I finish school. Maybe after I become an actress and famous I'll come back to where I used to live in a big car and pick up the people who used to take me around. But I don't know what will happen.

Puerto Ricans are also special people because they have special food like rice and beans. . . . I've been to Puerto Rico, and Puerto Ricans are nicer there. Maybe because it's so pretty there. The dances are different too and the food is different. The way they dress is different, and the customs are better there. It's nice here, but it's nice over there. Puerto Ricans there are very special people and they're different from others. Good different. The way they act and the way they treat each other. I think Puerto Ricans should know their history. I don't know Puerto Rican history, like I never learned it in school. But in my own way I know it.

THE YOUNG LORD

My NAME IS MARIO. I was born in 1950 in Spanish Harlem and my father was black and my mother was Puerto Rican. He was an alcoholic at the time and he still is. At the time I was born, they told him he was going to die from his liver problems but he didn't. He had become an alcoholic during World War II because he used to deal with syphilis cases, and there was no penicillin in those days so he used to have to do things like cut people's penises. He couldn't stand it and began drinking to make him forget. But by the end of the war he drank four to five quarts a day of wine. It wasn't hard for him to get it because he was a waiter. He used to try to do the right thing but the alcohol just wouldn't let him. It would get to him. He tried to beat my mother a few times but she could take pretty good care of herself and could stop him and she was okay. He was very unreliable because of his drinking. He would lose his job because he would disappear from it suddenly for two to three weeks while he went off and hit the bottle.

They were married for three years and then they had to separate. I stayed with my mother, and we got a three room flat in another part of town which is now torn down. It was a very Puerto Rican type environment and I was very Puerto Rican. I was always denounced for being black by my family because I was the blackest person in it. The majority of Puerto Ricans don't like blacks so it was a real hassle. There were other family problems besides. I'd see my father every two or three weeks, but sometimes he didn't show up for a long time if he was on one of his drinking binges. There were times he didn't show up for three or four years and then he'd come back and promise to reform, which he didn't. He'd soon start drinking. Wine, whiskey—whatever he could get his hands on.

I also had some problems with the Puerto Ricans in my neighborhood because of being black, so at the age of eight when I needed protection I joined a gang called "The Untouchables." By the age of nine I was already smoking reefers and it drove my mother crazy. I guess I was really quite advanced, because at the age of seven I had sex for the first time. I made it with my cousin. We were playing that old game of doctor and nurse. She was six years old. That may seem little, but I was little, so it fit with no problems. We kept making it together until I was twelve and then my mother caught me and I got my ass beat. I didn't run around with girls when I was twelve to fifteen, because I was too busy with my gang and spent most of my other time smoking.

At fifteen I learned how to make money off faggots, which was easy. Sometimes I got paid as much as fifty dollars if I would do anything they wanted me to. But I wouldn't go for the S & M scene [sadomasochism]. I met a couple of cats who wanted to beat me and shit, like that; but I just wasn't into that. Actually it wasn't all that easy to make money with faggots, because lots of them would try to get out of paying. A lot of times they tried to get away and I had to beat them up. Maybe that's what they wanted.

At thirteen I graduated Catholic school. I did a lot of drinking of wine and the gang wars stopped in the '60s and everybody got into the drug scene. I got heavier and heavier into reefers and I tried lots of other things, too, like mescaline, acid, downers, uppers, coke, STP. I started getting deeper into speed at fifteen, and finally I was sent to a hospital where I got detoxified for speed. It wasn't bad.

I dropped out of high school in my third year there. Actually I was kicked out because a teacher tried to hit me just for coming in late. Catholic schools are that way. So I hit him with a chair. He ended up in the hospital and I was almost sued as well. Although I didn't finish classes, I took the high school equivalency test and passed it.

Well, then the scene at home was pretty bad. My mother had remarried when I was three and my stepfather was a bummer. He had an authoritarian head and would always beat me with whatever he could find around —hands, belts, canes. It became the talk of the neighborhood how much I was getting beat. I had to get out of there, so at seventeen I left home and went into the air force, where I became a repairman. I was doing well, but then I had this fight with this guy. He called me a "nigger," so I put a chair on his head and he was sent to the hospital for eight months. He almost didn't make it.

Well, I got court martialed and was sentenced to two months hard labor in prison. It was very, very strict there. I was locked up sixteen hours a day, and the other eight I had to work my ass off. I got into a squabble with a guard, and the next thing I knew, they added another three months to my sentence. About a month of that I was put into solitary. The only way to keep your sanity during that is to talk to yourself and think about the things that happened to you in the past. It was about a four by eight room with only a little toilet where you shit. You were given food through a slot like a dangerous animal in a zoo. It was the regular army food, but sometimes I wouldn't eat it out of protest.

Anyway, I got out of the service about three years ago. I went back to the old neighborhood and didn't know what I was going to do for a while. But I knew the Chairman of the Young Lords, so I joined up with them. The Young Lords stood for liberation of Puerto Rico and liberation of the world. From my experience in the service and in jail, I had become politically conscious. But there were many things I didn't like about the Young Lords. Everybody there was so cold and unfriendly—they were into a real deep hate trip. They were always gossiping like little old ladies. They weren't really dealing with a revolutionary ideology—they were just gossiping all the time. While I was with them I became a Communist. In 1969 I went to Cuba for two months. I found it very heavy. There's still a lot of deep racism there. The majority who hold ranks are white Cubans. While I was in Cuba the FBI came to my house to check up on me with my parents but they said they didn't know where I was. They didn't. In the Young Lords I was in defense because I had a brown belt in karate. But we used more than just our hands for defense. We'd also use something called a *knunchakas*, which is two sticks attached with a rope. You can grab one end and swing the other and club someone with it without being that close to them. Maybe forty or fifty of the cats were in defense. In a rally or a demonstration we were like our own police. We needed a defense. So many people in the group were busted just for being in the group. We had our own clubhouse, and the police tried to mess around but we had our own lawyers. Sometimes we got after them. We used to get information from drug addicts on cops who would try to plant dope on people so they could bust them. So a bunch of us would jump him. They didn't mess around with us. But most of us were more afraid of them than they were of us.

I was part of the first church takeover. We got to the church at 11:30. At 11:40 Filippi got up to speak and said what his intentions were: he wanted a PE [Political Education] class and a breakfast program. In the middle of the speech, at about 11:50, forty-five to fifty cops came into the church. Forty of the Young Lords then got up and surrounded Filippi. And then the police started beating all of us. It was terrible. I was beaten for twenty minutes. I fought with nothing but my hands, although later they charged me with "assault with a weapon." And I knocked out a cop who later needed stitches. Filippi got his head cracked open. Thirteen of us were busted and the cop I knocked out later became my arresting officer.

They put four of us in a car and two tried to escape. The police ran out and caught both of them a block away. Then two more cops came in our car. One of them was the cop I had knocked out. I was bleeding heavily and very weak from the fight. But this cop pulled out his gun, pointed it at me, and said he wanted to shoot me right then and there. I really thought he would, but then his partner told him to like cool it. When I got into the precinct, though, he came after me and began to club me again. He sure wanted me. I spent five hours waiting to get to a hospital where I later had twenty-two stitches. I had to wait so long that the blood had clotted from the wounds. In court they threw everything at me and I got eight counts: felonious assault, assault and battery, criminal trespass, disrupting church services, assault with a weapon, disrupting governmental administration, riot, and disorderly conduct. The more stitches I had, the more charges they threw at me because they had to justify the beating they gave me.

I was taken to prison and I spent about six weeks there. It was very different from military prison because there were many more inmates. It was really depressing. I was finally bailed out, and the charges against me were dropped. After that I worked for the Sanitation Department for a while.

I was the type of cat that was raised in an environment and dug what was going on. I didn't fight it. I was also involved with the Panthers and with SNICK. But I got out of the Young Lords, because I realized it was a phony trip and it didn't mean anything and I was shedding my blood for nothing. For a while afterwards I started messing around with acid and snorting smack, but I was afraid to actually shoot it because I saw too many kids die that way.

Last year I became aware of Christ and stopped. And life is very different for me now. I used to hustle for money. I'd deal smoke. I'd sell grass by the pound. But when I became aware of Christ, I stopped. I didn't like the Catholic Church—the whole imperialistic trip in which they take vows of poverty and they're the richest church in the world. I also found that the average nun or priest was a sadist. I saw in school how much pleasure they got out of hitting kids. So I didn't go to the Catholic Church, but have my own church. It's my own thing. I believe in the Father, the Son, and the Holy Ghost. I ask them for wisdom, knowledge and understanding. Somehow I had gotten lost in the world. I think of myself as black, but I admit I have a Puerto Rican background. I have black friends, Puerto Rican, and white friends. I was real deep into the color thing in the service and when I was with the Young Lords, but now I'm out of it. I think I've found myself.

THE HAIRRAISER

My name is Tony. I was sad when I was told I had to come to America. My parents had come to America right after I was born and I lived with my grandparents in Puerto Rico until I was six. But then my parents sent for us from America, and my grandfather said, "Your mother wants you to come, so you've got to."

When we came here, we saw so many things we had never seen before. I had never been in a plane before. And that day was the first time I had worn shoes, but they were too tight because they belonged to someone with smaller feet. And my feet hurt so bad. . . . And on the plane these big kids grabbed me and my brother and made us get inside the bathroom. And once we went inside they locked us in from the outside. We were frightened until my brother saw that there was a lock inside so we were able to get out. But we felt bad, and wondered what we were getting into and what kind of people would be there.

I remember when I came to New York I saw that the

door to the building was open, and I asked my mother about it. But she showed me it was the doorway to the whole building and lots of other people lived there too. We just lived in one room, the four of us, and it was so crowded, and we all slept in the same bed. But I didn't mind because we had a TV. We never had a TV in Puerto Rico, and I didn't know what it was until my brother said, "Look, look, a TV!" And we put it on. Then I saw people talking there and having so much fun, and they had a big house like we had in Puerto Rico. So I went around to the back of the box to see if I could go into the house with them—but there was nothing there, and my brother and parents, they laughed at me.

I also remember that we had hot water. We had none in Puerto Rico, and the first time I turned it on I got bad burned. I began to scream and everyone laughed. I didn't know it would be hot. But then my brother, he done the same thing the next day, and I laughed.

I remember one time a colored fellow tried to rob the house. And a guy said, "Hold him, hold him!" And I was young, maybe ten years ago, but I held him. And everyone said, you know, "That boy is going to grow up to be something."

When I was in Puerto Rico I used to miss my parents, but when I came here I used to think about our big house and my grandparents, and I missed my grandfather so much. And one day we got a telegram and no one wanted to read it because we knew it was bad. My mother, she finally opened it and didn't say nothing to us. She just cried. And then my brother said, "Grandpa's dead." I missed my grandfather very much. I would often think even after he died that we'd play together one day again.

When he died, my grandmother came here also, and they left a little child they had living with them in Puerto Rico. She was my little cousin. I didn't never see her, and she was all alone in Puerto Rico.

My father and my mother, they've broken up several times. They always used to fight. Right after I was born my father left my mother for the first time. Then when I was about eighteen years old I decided to try to get to know my father. I really tried to get along with him, and I went to his house. He treated me real nice, like he liked me, and gave me money, and took me to places. One thing, though, my father wanted to make a boxer out of me and I didn't like it. He used to try to teach me to fight and would put gloves on us and then he would hit me. Not hard, you understand. And then he would tell me to hit him back. I couldn't though, because I was afraid I would hurt him and he wouldn't want to see me no more. But then he'd hit me harder and say, "Come on, come on." But I couldn't. And one day he hit me hard and I started crying, and he called me a sissy and said, "You ain't my son. You're a crying coward." He wanted to be proud of me, but I just don't like boxing.

I don't know why my father and mother split up, but I hear my father used to beat people bad. Like I heard one time he even tried to burn my mother. He tried to burn her back. That's what my mother told me. He got a bad temper. One time he tried to hit me, and I took a knife and told him I'd cut him real bad if he got near me. But my mother she held me. She wouldn't let me cut him, and she put me in back, so he hit her and not me.

He had two children from another wife—two girls— but I didn't know them till I was thirteen. One day my father came and showed me a picture of my other sister, and I said, "Oh, who is that beautiful girl?" And he said, "That's your sister." And I said, "Wow!" And then he said, "One of these days I'll come and get you so you and your brother can see your sister so you won't make a mistake. I don't want you to knock up your own sister." And then one day he took us to their house, and she was about fifteen, and I met her. Oh she was really beautiful. A beautiful girl, my sister. And he told me to make certain, like sure I wouldn't make a mistake and like try anything, because she was my sister and I couldn't marry her.

One day he won the numbers or something and just moved out. A month later he came back. He still had money left and my mother cried that she didn't want him. But she took him back for the money. She warned him, "One of these days I do to you what you did to me." And so the day he spent all his money and there wasn't nothing left, my mother said, "I'm paying you back." And we moved out and left him.

When I was about ten years old I used to have a bicycle and I used to love to ride it every place. And one day this little girl came over and asked me for a ride. I gave her a ride and then we went behind some cars. And that was the first time I started having sex. It's funny, no one told us, but I just knew what to do. Later I wondered how Adam and Eve knew how to do it. I guess you just know. I was a boy and she was a girl. She was about eight years old. I took her clothes off and we just started having sex.

I quit school in my first year of high school because I didn't like it. I wasn't learning anything. But I regret it now. I really regret it. I want to go back to school but

I think I'll have a lot of problems and trouble. They know the way I used to behave. I never used to try to learn nothing. And I got into a lot of trouble. I messed up everything because of the friends I used to have. If you wanted to be important, like you had to sass the teacher. Otherwise your friends would laugh and call you "sissy," or "queer." I used to play hookey a lot, because they'd say, "Come on, come on, let's go outside and play." I listened to them and that's how they got me in trouble.

When I quit school, my mother she felt very bad. She told me I was making a mistake. When I quit school I'd go out with my friends, hang around corners, and didn't do much. One time I went with these other boys, and they brung along two other girls. We went to a basement about two blocks from where we used to live and we lied down on the floor. We used our schoolbooks for a pillow. We told them they were our girls and we kissed them. Then we like, you know, sort of did it, and we were all doing it at once—trying to see which of us would come first. And the girls really liked it. But when we came out, this lady who knows my mother saw us. So my mother said she was going to send me to be with my father. And she tried to hit me, but I told her if she hit me, I hit her. So she didn't. But she asked why did I do that terrible thing with those girls, and I felt real bad. But I didn't stop.

I continued to play with these girls. Like one time my mother gave me money to get a hair cut, and I seen my girlfriend and other friends on the way and we went down to the basement and were, like, fooling around. About two hours after that we heard some noise, and the cops were there, and I know my mother reported me.

They caught us in the basement and took us to school. I didn't feel so good about the whole thing. When they came we were finished and just standing around talking. And the cops said, "What are you doing, sniffing glue?" And we said, "No," so they smelled our mouths. There wasn't no glue, but they warned us they might put us away in a reform school.

I knew a guy who was in a reform school and he told me it was no good. He said you got to do what they tell you to do, or they lock you away forever. Guys say they've been without a girl months and months, so whenever a person takes a shower they cannot bend down or they're liable to get fucked up the ass by somebody—somebody will try it and you won't know who it is. And like my friend who was in reform school, he says they missed girls so much, they been so long without a girl, that when they see Josephine the Plumber on television, they used to run to the bathroom and masturbate when they saw her. And like one time my cousin saw this guy masturbating and he had his finger up his ass. My cousin just stood there looking at him. And when the guy finished my cousin said, "Did you have fun?" And the guy got real scared and made him promise not to talk about it.

Sometimes I did sniff glue, and then I could be anything or anybody. I sniffed it because I liked the way I used to feel. I was about twelve or thirteen. It used to make me feel dizzy and I used to, like, dream. Some of the dreams were like real dreams—you know, like ways to make money. But others were funny. I once thought I was in this refrigerator and there was all this meat hanging there. I used to dream a lot of things—bad things, good things. I used to dream I was in a cage. And there were a lot of monkeys and things there

We used to go into basements and take a paperbag and make it like a hat and then put the glue inside the bag. Then we'd put it over our faces and sniff. We stole the money for the glue. Some I stole from my mother and brother. But they didn't have much, so we used to go to this gym where I used to go swimming. We'd go into the locker room because nobody was ever there, and then we'd steal money if we found it. I used to be a real bad boy at that time but when I got older, I started being nice to my mother and started behaving. I don't know why. Maybe it was because I was getting older. That's when I stopped sniffing glue. I realized I wasn't getting nothing out of it and I knew it wasn't good for my health. Because one day this lady, a friend of my mother, she took me to see a film about it, and the film shows what glue does to your lungs and then I didn't want no more glue.

When I was fourteen or fifteen I used to smoke pot. I thought it made me a big man. Not a little fourteen-year-old that someone could push around. I was working then, and had plenty of money to buy it. It used to make me happy and it made me laugh. I used to see things different —like different colors, and I'd hear things differently—I'd hear music more clear. And I used to like to look at the TV and I would understand it better from normally. I stopped after I went to Puerto Rico for a while, because I didn't use it over there. And I realized that I didn't need it any-more; it just wasn't doing nothing for me.

I tripped three times on LSD. I stopped fast, because it's really no good. It's really bad for your mind and you get high for too many hours and it's too long before the high goes away. You see all sorts of strange things when you take it—like a car coming at you, or people coming into rooms when there's no one there. And you start laughing a lot—even if someone gets hurt you laugh, and that's not right.

But heroin I'd never try, never. Because of what it does to you. The other day I was looking out the window and it was raining real bad like you wouldn't want to go out nowhere and I could see the dope guys walking in the street, getting all wet in the rain, looking for the money to buy heroin. These guys walk in the rain and the snow to get money to buy a shot. I don't know what happens to people who take it, they become different people. They look like . . . I don't know . . . very different. None of my relatives take nothing that I know of. We're too smart. You know why they call it dope? Because it's for dopes. The name tells you everything: Dope.

I used to belong to a gang called the Hairraisers. I don't know where the name came from, but that was what we called ourselves. I was about thirteen at the time, and all we did was get into fights. We used to fight kids from other places who were coming into our territory. I never really got hurt but some of the others did. I remember one time I hit a kid on the head with a rock. I was running and he was running after me with a whole bunch of guys and I really got scared. Suddenly I picked up a rock and I shouted, "The first guy who shows his head I'm going to hit him." And then this stupid guy showed his head. I remember the moment I hit him. He started yelling, "Ay! Ay!" I looked back to see if he was bleeding, but I really don't know if I killed him, or what. Sometimes I feel bad about it—I try to sleep and then I think, maybe

I killed a guy. For many weeks after that I was waiting for the police to come and put me in jail forever, or maybe even kill me.

Once, when I was with our gang, I saw this girl who had her eye blown out with a rock. It started bleeding and all that. We were all inside a car. We went into another gang's territory, and we kept screaming, "Hairraiser! Hairraiser!" And then we went around the corner, and this time the light was red and we had to stop. And the other gang were waiting for us. They started throwing rocks at us, and then all of a sudden they hit this girl who was with us, and took her eye right out. And then the car crashed into a tree and we took her out of the car real fast and put her into a hallway and called an ambulance. We didn't wait for the ambulance because we didn't want to get no trouble, and we ran away fast. I never saw her again; I don't know what happened to her.

Sometimes I pray for her in church. I pray for my family in the nighttime, too, every night before I go to sleep. I pray quietly. I know God helps me a lot. I figure he tried to keep me away from trouble and everything like that. Like, trying not to be a junkie, and sometimes I ask him for that, and I ask him to help me be nice to my mother. I try to be good to other people.

Right now I wish I were back in regular school. I had fun when I first quit school, but right now I really regret I'm out of it. What I really want to be, I can't be. I really want to be an electrician. They earn good money. I know, because a friend of mine was an electrician and I used to see how he had all this money all the time.

I'd like to go back to Puerto Rico, but first I want to get a job, a skill. Then I can go back to Puerto Rico, because I like it down there. I've got friends and family there—it's my country. I'd like to live down there, because here all I got is my mother. Everybody is back there. My brother's back there now, and even father is in Puerto Rico with his new wife.

Someday I really hope to go to Puerto Rico with my family and live in a house again. I'd like to live with my mother, my sister, and my brother, and I wish we could have a house and a car. That's what I wish for. I'd like to stay there and live forever. And I'd like to get married. I'd like to marry a girl from my own country. She could be poor or rich, it doesn't matter—so long as she likes me and I love her.

THE NEWCOMER

My name is Maria. I was born in Puerto Rico and I have one brother. I have a mother and a father and my father was the boss. When I was about a year old my mother and father separated. I don't know why. He came to America after he left her. I saw him only once when I was expecting my baby. He came to see it. I didn't think nothing of it because I don't love him. He sent me money for school, but money isn't love.

My mother and I stayed in Puerto Rico for many years and I went to a Catholic school. It was run by nuns. I like Puerto Rico much better than New York. In Puerto Rico you've got no problems with colors. It doesn't matter what color a person is. You don't have problems with street gangs and fights like you do here, and I never saw anyone take drugs in Puerto Rico. There was no problem there about walking in the street late at night— there you could do it all the time, but here it's hard socially because you can't go out at night alone. I never saw little girls smoking in Puerto Rico but here I've seen girls smoking at four or five years old. I think it's silly. Here people dress funny, and you don't know if you're looking at a man or a woman.

We also have to pay too much rent here. Everything you earn goes to pay for a terrible apartment. In Puerto Rico my mother spent fifty dollars for five rooms and here we spend a hundred for two rooms. It's also expensive to dress in America. In Puerto Rico we would wear the same clothes all the time. Nobody thought it funny if you always wore the same few dresses, so long as they were clean. But here they whisper about you if you wear the same thing, so you have to buy a different dress for every day and you might not wear a dress more than a few times a year. It's a waste of money.

And there's too many blacks here. I don't like blacks. They're not like Puerto Ricans. If you need something, they won't help you. Puerto Ricans will do everything for you. And when I go on the subway, I hear blacks say bad things about Puerto Ricans, like we don't teach our kids English. And Americans confuse blacks for Puerto Ricans, although we're very different. If a black does something bad, or anything happens, they say it's a Puerto Rican who did it. I don't like this country.

I started dating in Puerto Rico when I was fourteen, and I met my first husband at a wedding. We danced all evening and he asked to see me again, so I said, "I'll have to ask my mother." That was the way we did it in Puerto Rico, but they don't do it that way here. So my mother said okay, if he comes in and sees me, so we saw each other. Then we got married. But his parents didn't like me. They never did, because I don't have a father and they're Catholic. That's the only reason I can think of. We never did anything wrong—I never slept with him until I married him. But here in New York, the men want you to sleep with them first. That's wrong.

It was a nice marriage. I didn't do any birth control and had my first baby in nine months. We came up here, and he was studying to be a policeman. Then he wanted to go back to Puerto Rico, and I asked my mother if I had to. And she said, "You have to follow your husband." So I did. He worked at the police department. Then one day I find a piece of paper in a book of his and it's got a girl's name on it and also her telephone number. I called her up and asked if she knew my husband and she said she did. I asked her, "Is he your boyfriend?" And she said, "Yes." I said, "He can't be your boyfriend, because he's married to me." And she said, "He isn't married. He told me so." So I said, "If you don't believe me, come and see his baby and see if he isn't married."

She came and was very fresh. She was from New York. I showed her the four-month-old baby but she still didn't believe we were married. So I showed her my wedding pictures. Then she believed me.

One day he asked for a divorce so he could marry her and I asked my mother what I should do. She said I didn't have to give him a divorce, and I should leave Puerto Rico. So I did. I came here with my baby and he stayed in Puerto Rico. And one day I got a letter from him saying we are divorced. I don't know how he got it, but when I went down to visit Puerto Rico I went to court to see if we were divorced and I saw in the court papers we were. The other girl, she was pregnant and then had a child like mine. I was twenty-two. My husband, he loved me too much—but his father didn't. His father said if he divorced me, he'd have a big house. So he divorced me and he has a big house.

I wanted to go back to Puerto Rico, but I'm afraid that if I do he'll steal the baby. He writes and tells me he wants to. I write him back and say, "Try." And if I live here, he can't have the child on weekends. I don't want him to be able to see his child because he was bad with me. It doesn't matter to the child. He sends it forty dollars a month. But I don't think he loves it—he's just glad it's a boy. If it was a girl he wouldn't want it.

So I went to work in a factory and I met a boy. And after I talked to him two times, I told him that I don't like being alone here, and that I'm a nice girl and I don't smoke or dance. And I told him I have a boy and does he want to marry me? So we got married. I love him and get along with him, and I'm happy. I make a hundred twenty-seven dollars and he makes a hundred as a cashier in a supermarket. We have one child now, too, and I don't want to have any more children because it's too expensive, and if I have any more, I can't work. They grow up so differently in America ·No one cares here. If you're run over by a car no one would even look for you. If you ask people for directions, they tell you the wrong way. I want my children to be brought up in Puerto Rico. It's too dangerous to grow up here, with all that killing. And the drugs—that's the really big problem. If you're working, you don't know what they're doing and bad things can happen. I have about three hundred dollars saved up. I want to save up five thousand, and that'll take me about three more years. Then I'll go back to Puerto Rico and bring up my two children. That's the best way.

THE HUSTLER

My NAME IS RICKY and I'm Puerto Rican. The best thing thing about being Puerto Rican is just being Puerto Rican. That's where it's at. I believe Puerto Rican people are the best cause they're my breed. They treat me very good —very good. Like they ain't cheap with their stuff. Say you're at a party and it's late. And they say right away, "We got an extra bed. Sleep here." And they feed you and they do everything for you. And they don't have that much. But they've always given to everyone, and they'll give you what they got because they're generous.

Where I live now it looks like a ghetto. But it used to be real pretty. When I was young there were no addicts there and nobody was uptight about drugs. Now everybody is, because there's a lot of junkies hanging around all over the neighborhood. Puerto Ricans. Blacks. Dominicans. All the races mix. It don't matter. But now there's real trouble because the Dominicans are trying to take over—they're trying to be the big bosses of the block. But the Negroes and Puerto Ricans won't let them. We won't bother them, but when they start something we sure as hell try to finish it. They're scared too. They never fight by themselves and don't start anything unless they have their friends around. So you can always tell when they're going to start a fight cause there's a bunch of them together. So if they're going to have a rumble, then the Puerto Ricans go out and get their friends too.

Around my way, there's a lot of gangs. Mostly everybody belongs to a gang. They're big clicks too. Dominican gangs have about four hundred kids from here and more in New Jersey. There's only one Dominican gang, the Saints. But I'm not a member of a gang. Guys join gangs because they have to have protection. But I'm pretty tough myself—I consider myself tough. I'm not scaring anybody, mind you, but like dig it, I mind my own business. I really don't go out and look for trouble. Some people look for trouble I guess because they want to be big. I don't need it; I'm where I want to be at now.

But I've seen gang fights. The guys fight with clubs, pipes—anything they can get their hands on. But the Saints, they use guns all the time. They had a good fight I saw once. They were beating this guy up. I don't know why—maybe they were trying to shake him down for money, or maybe he was a stoolie on dope. But they beat him up real bad—seven or eight guys against this one. But the next night the guy who got beat up comes out again and calls over one of the guys who beat him up. And as soon as that guy got close to him, he took out his gun and emptied four bullets right into him. He shot him good. That guy who got shot was one of the bad guys, so I'm glad it happened to him. He was taking off on everybody. Christ—he used to rob everybody, even his mother. This guy got shot in the stomach, and he looked around, like, "Wha happened?" and then he just dropped right then. But he didn't die, maybe because he got to a hospital fast.

There's a lot of violence where I live. Like one time I remember there were six cars filled with Dominicans with guns. At first they were fighting with everything else —sticks, stones, even throwing garbage cans. But then there was some shooting. After a while it cooled off. I watch not because I'm interested, but because you got no choice. After all, if I'm there, what am I going to do —just look the other way? But I like to see people who deserve to get hurt get theirs, you know? The guys that hurt other people. Like the junkies—most people who get hurt in these fights are junkies, because they're the ones who go around hurting people and the others get even. They mug people, kill people and rob houses, and the people around my way they don't got that much. Maybe they save a year for a television set, and they enjoy watching it. And then here comes somebody, some punk little junkie after a little bag, and they rob these people and take all they've got and leave them with nothing.

I know a whole lot of junkies, but they're not my friends—I don't hang out with them. I don't know how people become junkies in the first place. Maybe they're influenced by their friends or they pick it up in school— but something happens to them.

The first time I came across drugs it was a long time ago when I was eleven years old. I went on the roof to check out my friend's birds. He had a coop of all kinds of pigeons. And I see this guy shooting up, and the whole thing. It was a bad scene.

I never smoked marijuana cause I don't need it. I don't need anything. When I was little maybe, yes; but now that I'm sixteen, no. Maybe other people need to feel nice. Maybe it makes them feel like a big man. It's the same with violence, guns, and killings I guess.

I feel nice when I shoot pool. I'm pretty damned good too. I make money from it, in fact. I can make thirty or forty dollars on a weekend. I just go up to a guy and say, "Hey, do you want to shoot pool?" I lose a lot of times, but I've won more money than I lost. And I also like to play poker. The worst I ever hurt somebody was when I was playing stud poker with this dude who was trying to cheat. He wanted to take all the money in the pot by taking cards from the bottom. I checked them out, and other people checked them out—and sure enough, he was cheating like shit. Then he pushed me, and the next thing I know I hit him with a chair. I knocked him down on the floor and he was bleeding bad. And then I took my money and left. I don't know what happened, man—I think I hurt him bad, but I ain't sorry. Who told him to cheat? I'd do it again to anybody who tries to cheat.

Another thing I've always liked to do is turn on the fire hydrant, and then take a can and play. It's fun getting wet and running around getting other people wet. One time when I was little I was playing with the fire hydrant and I was covering myself with a box so I didn't see a car coming. And I guess the car didn't see me either and the driver didn't pay any attention to the water and I got hit. That happened twice more. The person that hit me the third time was my lawyer. He was going to my house to talk to my parents about the first two cases and then he hit me. I tried to sue but I don't know what happened. I wasn't hurt bad.

I'd still like to play with the fire hydrant, but the cops picked me up for opening one last summer. Did you ever get your ass kicked by a cop? I did. Boy it was real bad. They just looked me over, and the next thing I know, I was getting beat up by two of them. They left me there about two miles from my house and I could hardly walk. I had to walk back, though, cause I didn't have the money to ride.

The only other time I got into trouble with the police was once when they asked me my name. I gave them a phony name and a phony address. I told them I didn't have a phone number, and they believed me. Boy are they stupid.

Some of these cops, man, they're really out to get you. The shit is they won't bust the main people. Did you read about junkies, and how they don't even go to jail now? Like for me, if I walked out of here with a joint in my hand, I'd be killed. Especially two cops around my block, boy they're real bad. We call them Cowboy and Indian. This guy Cowboy is a tall guy, and he's a real mean dude. And Indian, he don't take no shit from nobody. They're partners. These guys are too much. I ain't got nothing really against them, mind you. I'm just saying they're really ball busters.

When a cop gets shot, I say that's bad. Like, they have to take care of people and they're just people too. They weren't born cops, they just got in it. In fact, I like Puerto Rican cops. They're together people. My brother knows a Puerto Rican cop. The other day he came up to a birthday party for my sister. He was so high, man—like he was stoned out of his mind. He's real cool people. He used to go out with my sister. Now he gangs out with my brother. My brother smokes, and I think he snorts coke also. I don't know about the cop but I wouldn't put it past him.

I've never gotten into trouble with cops over smoking and my girlfriend hasn't neither and she smokes too. I've got a regular girl. I've been going with her almost a year. I started going out with girls when I was about ten years old, but I didn't do anything then. We used to hang out in the building. Me and this girl stayed together for about a month and a half. Then I was tired of her. When I was about thirteen, that was the first time I ever had a chick —you know, screwed her. She was a good lay. She was about sixteen at the time and we were making it together real good. But then she broke up with me because she felt bad because she was older than me. She split but I've always still liked her.

I don't score with my girl now. I just don't mess around here, around my way. I'll go with my friend some place far away and get it. It's pretty easy. Girls think I'm pretty sharp looking, and I rap with them and they always like that. But I don't waste time rapping with a chick if I don't think I'll get any pussy. But I don't go for prostitutes. Ever. Girls try to pick me up but I know they probably did something wrong and probably got the syph anyway, so I wouldn't bother. A lot of these girls are junkies, and they changed because of drugs. They needed the money for drugs so they had to sell their bodies. And then their figures and their faces changed and the way they look changed. They don't wear no more makeup and their clothes are all raggedy and they're dirty. I don't feel sorry for them, though. I used to but not no more—they messed themselves up because they hanged around with the wrong guys. And I stayed away from them.

I like the fact that Puerto Ricans are not really quiet and also that they're clean. In Puerto Rico they take baths two times a day. When I go there I'm embarrassed, because I don't. I don't know, but they change when they come over here. They talk different and lose their habits —mostly their good habits. They're not as clean or as good here. But Puerto Ricans are proud and that's good. Maybe that's why we fight a lot. We are proud people and we don't take anything off of people. We don't ask nobody for nothing. If I had no money I wouldn't ask anybody— I wouldn't even borrow money off my friends. That how proud I am.

I used to be really prejudiced against white people. I really hated white people. I used to hate Italians. Actually, until I was in high school I used to hate all kinds of white people, like Jews. And then I realized that I didn't know what kind of people they were, and I really found out they're cool people.

But the Dominicans, I can't stand them. Those people are too much. They're very rowdy and loud. They're really dirty. But mainly they're vulgar. I don't know any Dominicans because I don't associate with those kinds of people. The only one I can stand is my girl's sister's husband—he's a Dominican, but he's cool people. The rest is these loud and weird people.

I got a lot of black friends and they're pretty cool. They're cool people. Maybe Dominicans and Puerto Ricans don't get together because they're both Latin, and they got their different ways of doing things. But blacks,

like they understand what's happening. But these Dominicans are garbage.

I don't think I'm prejudiced really, because prejudice
is hate and I don't hate anybody. I just get angry sometimes. I've been angry so many times. Christ—I'm angry
every day. The slightest thing that bothers me makes me
mad. I don't know what it is. When I get angry I try to go
someplace to cool off, because otherwise . . . Sometimes
I hit people. Once I banged my girl right in the chest so
hard that she fell on the floor. I smacked her pretty hard
because I was stoned. I was drinking Johnny Walker and
wine or something, and she was arguing about something.
Then she hit my arm. The next thing I know my arm went
flying. I didn't mean to hit her—my arm just went
flying. Then I felt bad, cause she was crying. So I tell her,
"I'm sorry," and shit like that, and I said, "Be cool." And
she understood. And everything was all right.

I've hit a lot of girls, I guess, when they did something wrong. Like, if I tell them not to do something and
they go ahead and do it, the next thing I know I'm
slapping them round because I'm mad. But I don't think
girls really mind it, although they say they do. And that's
when they learn. Once I hit a girl, she never does it again
while she's going out with me. When a chick is going out
with me, she's home all the time. I'm the one who has got
to take her out. I mean, I let them go out with their
mother, but I wouldn't let them run around with no guys.
If I say, "I don't want you there," she'd better not go
there. Because if I catch her there, she's going to get
hurt.

The only time I don't get mad ever is when I'm
smoking. I smoke every day because it don't cost me

nothing. I get it free, because I know a lot of people with connections. And they get it by the pound and they give me some to sell and I make two dollars a bag. Around my way, if you got a good smoke they don't give you that much. They give you enough for four or five joints, because one Colombian will knock you out. And I got Colombian—good pure Colombian. Half a joint will knock you out. It's real dynamite. For five dollars guys wait for me on the way to school so they can buy from me because they know I've got the best. I only deal in school. One time they almost caught me but I saw them coming and I put the bags in my socks. They came over to me real tough like, and told me to take everything out of my pockets. I was trying very hard to be cool, but I was really scared shit. I tried not to even perspire cause that can give you away just like your face. So I told my body not to sweat. And they didn't find it and they were mad. They wanted to bust me and get the bad apples out of school.

All I do is smoke and smoke. Today I sold three packs besides. I get my stuff from a forty-year-old Dominican. A real fag—boy, is he queer. I think my brother maybe messed around with him. Man I smoke myself every day. Like tonight we're having a real big party. Friday night we just lay out the joints, and we smoke and use combustion tubes. That's a little glass tube. You hold it and the smoke goes in and you suck it in and it goes right down. All the smoke goes down you real fast. If you take too much, though, you choke and cough. . . .

I pray to God not to get caught. When I'm in a real jam, I pray. I believe in God. The last time I prayed to him was when I was afraid my mother would find some of my bags. I had hidden them in the apartment and one day she said she was going to clean the place up the next day. And she didn't go out, so I couldn't get them out. So I prayed that she wouldn't find them. I was really scared. I think God helped then. I think he really answered my prayers, because she didn't find them. I figure God thinks marijuana is like smoking and drinking —there's nothing bad about it. It goes back to the Egyptians B.C. People have been snorting to get funny feelings always.

I plan to get married someday and have a family. I plan to get engaged next year. But the girl I marry has got to be a virgin. Nothing but a virgin—and if she's lying I'll know it. Because I don't want a girl whose been popped before. That's my job for my wife. Maybe other people think differently; but my wife, she's gotta be a virgin.

When we have a family, I want a boy first, so I can name it after me. Then he'll be the man of the house when I'm not around, and when I'm around, we'll take care of each other. I'll take him in the street and teach him what's right and wrong about everything. That won't be my wife's job. I've got other things for her to do. You know what I like best about my chick? She understands me. She knows what I like and what I don't like. She knows what I think. She only knows me for eleven months, but she knows everything about me. I think that's love. Like, if I felt like screwing a girl, my chick is so beautiful I wouldn't go up to her. I'd save her for last. The best. I'd go up to some other girl and do it with them. That's love.

But I also liked the chicks in Puerto Rico. Not like

my girl, understand, but the girls there are very pretty and they all have great shapes. All of them. I don't know why. I haven't figured it out myself. But they all have great shapes, man. They know how to dress, how to dance, how to do everything. They know how to enjoy themselves. Make you feel good. When you go over there, man, they treat you real nice. That's Puerto Rico.

THE PROUD ONE

MY NAME IS CARMELITA. My father was middle aged when he came here from Puerto Rico and my mother was young. My father came here first and stayed for a few months before he sent for my mother and brother. At first they lived in a very small furnished room. My father couldn't find a job and he was very unhappy. His pride was hurt. I wasn't born yet but my mother tells me he changed. Then my father got into the gambling thing, and that's how he supported himself, and then supported a family. He was a good gambler; he made money and then he got a job, but there still really wasn't enough money. As we grew up, we didn't have everything in life, but it wasn't bad. There were many things we wanted, but there were four of us in the family.

My father gambled mostly with other Puerto Ricans. Craps, cards, but then he got a job working at a school. I don't really know what he did. And that was all for him. He had his job and he was scared to do anything different.

He worked there for twenty years and then he retired.

I don't remember how much he earned but it wasn't enough to have everything in life. We had a run-down old television we bought from a family we knew, and we had some living room furniture and we had beds. But as far as us going to the movies or anything like that, we never had the money.

When I was little I was scared of blacks. Sometimes we'd have fights and call each other names relating to race. They would call us spic. I even remember the first time I heard that word. It was a long time ago. And I stopped being afraid of them when I moved to a new neighborhood. Mostly blacks lived there, and I went to school with a lot of blacks. I was scared of some of them. They would pull my hair, but I'd talk back to them—I just stood up to them.

I got into trouble once in school fighting with a Negro girl. I was in the seventh grade, and I had a friend who had a very bad heart, a heart murmur. She was quiet and much more timid than I was. She had to be, and I was sticking up for her. Some girl started bothering her and pulling her hair. She was ugly and fat and she started up with her, so I hit her with my fist. We were in the orchestra, and I had a clarinet in my hand, and when she came back I hit her in the head with my clarinet. I think we fought because she was black and we were Puerto Rican and she was jealous.

Even before that, she used to call my mother a whore in front of the class and she'd say anything to make me embarrassed. Anyway, we got in a big thing, and the teacher tried to stop the fight and held me back and she came towards me, so I bit the teacher. They took me to the principal's office. I guess the only reason I wasn't expelled was because I was a good student. It was an honor class and that was my first fight, the first time I really got in trouble. The teacher knew me very well. My brother went to that school and I guess they knew we weren't that type. So they gave me another chance.

My brother is older than I am. He was born in Puerto Rico, and moving here affected him a lot. There were a lot of gangs. He wasn't in a gang himself, but he was always involved with them because his friends were in gangs. In fact he was a good student. He always pulled very good grades. He wanted to be a doctor but the counselor at school said no. He felt very bad. He was in an honor class, but they just didn't feel he could be a doctor. He always tried to do better, he tried as hard as he could, but they told him he couldn't make it.

I started working very young. I was about ten years old, when I started working. I worked at a small store and I sold things. A Negro man owned the store. He hired me because he saw me in the store a few times and he liked the way I talked and the way I dressed. I never bought anything there. I mostly made my own clothes. He offered me the job, but since I was so very young he said he'd keep me off the books.

Later I went to work for a Jewish man, a dry cleaner, and I did books for him and things like that. I worked every day after school and Friday until late—ten o'clock. Saturdays I worked, too, and holidays I worked very, very late.

I went out a lot. But I was most interested in dressing up because at the time it was the thing everybody did. You know, it was important to look good and I knew I wouldn't be able to dress like that when I got married.

When I dressed good it made me feel good. Knowing that I was earning and I could afford to buy them for myself also made me feel good—knowing that I didn't have to ask my father for them because I knew maybe he'd give me the money when he really couldn't afford it and should have used it for something else. I love him and he loved me a whole lot, and he might have given me almost anything I wanted, because I was a girl and he figured if I'd get desperate I'd do something. He loves me that much. So I really felt I had to do it for myself if I wanted that.

When I told him I wanted to work, he didn't like it. He got very mad and I had to go to work without his permission. My mother thought it was a good idea, and she helped me. But he never approved. When I came home late from work my father would say cruel words. He never liked it. But after I finished high school I had time for work. But he was always very angry, he just didn't want me to. Finally my parents separated, so he had no say. I was about, oh, fourteen, when they separated. Or maybe a little younger. I don't remember exactly. I guess it was mostly over financial problems, really. He didn't want my mother to work either. He was much older than my mother and very jealous. My mother being a woman wanted to buy things and he couldn't afford them. First thing, money went to buy food and things like that. And she figured she was never going to go anyplace. There was no future. My father was a stubborn man and they fought, and then they broke up.

Puerto Rican families are very strict. The men are very possessive of their women and very conscious of what they look like, things like that. My father was strict with me. He was that type of man, but he never threatened me or anything like that. He was strict with himself too. He never smoked or drank—I don't think I ever saw a bottle of beer in my house. He was against all that. He was very strict and very stubborn. The old ways were his own ways. I never smoked. My brother tried to smoke at night. He felt that it was better to do it out in the open, but my father wouldn't give him any money for cigarettes and my mother got very annoyed. She said if my father wouldn't give him the money he might do something drastic to get it. Then my father would get angry and when he got angry he would yell. He yelled a lot. He had a loud voice— when he whispers he sounds like he's yelling. He never really talked to us. He yelled like he was giving orders; he was the man. She couldn't talk to him and she never liked that. My brother used to argue with him a lot. My only argument was that he wouldn't let me go out much.

My father felt that every man I knew in the street was either a bum or a criminal. There just wasn't anybody good enough for me. At that time there were a lot of gang wars and fighting, especially in our neighborhood. He didn't like any of them. He said if they lived in our neighborhood, they couldn't be too good. And when I went downstairs, like forget it. He would come down and watch When I really did a lot of dating, I was older and he was already out of the house, so it wasn't that bad.

I did once have a problem with a boy. His name was Joey. He threatened me. Now he's in jail for attempted rape and attempted murder. When I had the problem with him it was very embarrassing, and during this incident and just before it my father used to follow me, to make sure nothing happened. It was bad. What happened was I got involved and while I was dating him he got involved with drugs. He was sent upstate and I thought I got rid of him. He was Puerto Rican. His family background was very bad. His father was killed in a knife fight. He sort of wanted to carry this on, and he got into trouble. He became very possessive of me. He would beat me up if I wouldn't say I was his girl and be with him. I mean I was like thirteen, and I just didn't want to get involved. But he threatened me. He knew where I was at and he would follow me.

My father used to be afraid for me. He warned him that he would call the police if he didn't behave. The last time I saw Joey I remember it was Thanksgiving Day. I hadn't seen him in a while. I saw him in the street when I was walking with a girl friend. He said he wanted to speak to me. I said no, but he forced me into a building— I went with him because he had a knife. I tried crying and he said he wanted to go out with me again. I said I would think about it. I just wanted to get out of there. I told him to let me leave the building and I would think about it. He hit me but he never, not even then, tried to manhandle me or rape me. He never did anything like that to me. He just wanted me to stay with him. He used to say that if I didn't want to be his girl, nobody could be his girl. And if I wasn't his, I'd be nobody's—he'd make sure of that. By that, I knew he meant he'd ruin or disfigure my face or that he'd ruin my pride. I was very scared. I ran back out in the street and then I saw my girl friend was looking at me. And I was all messy from crying and crying.

I thought he had left, but he came again with some guy he said had just gotten out of jail for murder, or something, and the guy tried to stab me. He lifted up his hand and I saw a knife and I screamed. And then I jumped, and the knife hit the wall. I would have been hit in the stomach if I hadn't jumped, I think. And I started screaming and screaming. Then they ran off. They just ran right down the block. And I never saw him after that. Then later he got sent to jail.

When I first started seeing Joey I liked him. He wasn't on drugs then. He didn't go to school. He was involved in gangs and things like that so they kept sending him to correction school and places like that. When he came back, he was using drugs. He used heroin. He was a mainliner. And I just couldn't take the idea. His character changed. He was getting too possessive and when he was using heroin I just couldn't breathe. I couldn't do anything.

This was also when he started getting very violent. He just didn't seem to give a damn. He'd get money for what he wanted. He'd lie and steal. But he never asked me for money, never. In fact, he used to talk about us getting married young. I used to wonder how he could support us. But I just couldn't see myself in that kind of life—running. So much of the time he was a fugitive. They were looking for him. That's no kind of a life. That's no life for me.

Drugs were used in junior high school. Glue sniffing was a very cheap high. I tried it, but I didn't like it. It was more like a bzzz feeling. Bong. King of the world. But I just didn't like it. It gave me a pale look. That's the God's honest truth. But I did it to keep up with everybody. I didn't think it could hurt me. Nobody really said anything about it; where I lived it was considered nothing.

When I was a girl, they never talked about drugs in school. People did it in school because it was so easy to do. You would go in a hall between classes, or go to the bathroom and do it. Nobody looked. Nobody checked. It was so easy. You just go take out a bag and put a little glue in it and sniff it quick. Who the hell's going to know? And then you go back to class like nothing ever happened. When I was in high school they used to do it in the classroom. And a lot of the teachers were ignorant—but they couldn't be *that* ignorant. I don't know. They just wouldn't say anything.

The other drugs were marijuana; heroin for some people. You saw a lot of marijuana around school, but not in school because it gave off a smell. You could do it in the park, someplace where it wouldn't attract people. I was never really offered any because there was a group of fellows, who, well, they thought I was really something special. Some of them were friends of my brother, and they said they'd actually kill me if I did anything like that.

I remember one fellow, a Negro fellow, and one day he asked me, very friendly, if I wanted to make some money. And I was very interested. I was very young, and I figured the money would come in handy. So he said he would give me marijuana to sell, but then I realized he was just pretending. If I had said yes, he would have slapped me across the mouth and taken me to my mother's house and told her. So I said no. Then he told me he was just testing me. I really learned a lot from that. He said I didn't know what it was like to be taking drugs, and what it was like to be in jail. He'd been in jail, but not for long. He really wasn't a pusher. He was an athlete and a friend.

I remember he took me around and he showed me. He showed me a couple of girls, and later I did the same thing to another girl. I showed her. He made me realize that I would look like them. He took me to West 111th

Street and Lenox Avenue and there I met a girl I had known. The girl used to be very beautiful and always dressed so nicely. But when I saw her, she was hustling for her habit. She looked terrible. She was like two years older than me. She was about sixteen, really, like wow, I thought. But now she looked like a hard woman, you know what I mean? Like hard. You could tell what kind of a girl she was. Dirty. This was the summertime and she looked and smelled like she never took a bath.

And the crowd that she was with, man. They weren't fellows her age, they were older men, it was really a disgusting sight. They were all ragged bums, Puerto Ricans, well anyway they were Spanish, and blacks. And the guy that took me there was saying, "Remember her? She's on heroin." I felt so sorry for her. She recognized me. She said "Hi, how are you doing?" But then she said she had to go. And I knew she was hustling to try to get the money for a high. I felt really bad, but I had no pity for her—she could have really been nice.

When I was very young there were a lot of gangs. They were everywhere I used to go. Their names used to come out of the newspapers, names like Sports, Dragon, names like that. And these gangs were always trying to keep other people from coming into their territory. There was a lot of antenna fights, and they had brass knuckles and things like that. They were supposed to be fair fights. One on one, with three guys backing each of them up— fighting it out equally. But it didn't last. They'd have extra gang members looking out, to see if they needed them, and the other gang would do the same, so before you knew it they'd all be there. It was bloody, but not that bloody. It could have been a lot worse if they had guns. But luckily they didn't have guns—they had antennas. One guy got his finger cut off.

Most of these gang fights occurred in the summer. Nobody got arrested because that's one thing about being in a gang: they look out for each other. They see a cop coming, and they'll even tell a guy in another gang: "Cop's coming." There were two main gangs, both Puerto Rican, though there were some Blacks and Italians in them. They were mostly fighting over territory: each gang thought their territory belonged to them, and they figured nobody else had reason to come there. And then a guy'd come from another area. He'd come down the street bopping— it's a slang word that means a tough way of walking, it's like you're hot shit. And a guy would come walking like that and one of them would say, "Look at that guy bopping in our territory. He's looking for trouble." And so on, until they'd get a couple of fellows and a fight would occur.

Also, at dances, both gangs were invited, and one wrong move—you trip, you bump—and they'd start a big thing about it. Once I got in the middle. I got hysterical and I didn't know what to do. So then they just pushed me away. And then they started fighting. I was crying, because I didn't want nothing to happen. That was the only one I was really near.

The other fight I saw outside my window. Every time I looked out I heard screaming, and I thought someone was going to die. I was really terrified, and then when the cops came, I figured I was going to get involved in something I wasn't even in. But later I met up with two of the fellows involved. One of them showed me his hand and it was bloody. I thought the whole thing was kind of stupid.

It all happened just because of pride. Otherwise they could talk it out and try to prevent it. But because you've got pride you say, "No, that's not going to go with my head, I'm going to show them I'm a man." And because of that pride, that's the main reason they fight.

A lot of the girls were being used, but I didn't care for that. If they think you're a very nice girl, that's the way they're going to treat you. If they think you're a girl from the street, then that's how they'll treat you—like someone from the street. They date you once, get what they can get out of you, and they'll do it. But if a girl shows respect for herself, I guess that's what they like.

It's like me. I wouldn't go out with everybody, and I guess they figure if they have a tough time getting me to go out with them, I have pride. I never experienced anything bad because of that. I had a lot of pride. I cared about myself. Other girls just didn't care about their reputations. They slept with every Tom, Dick or Harry and maybe they thought it made them look like something. I never thought about it that way. We talked about it, girls about my age, thirteen or a little older. And some girls thought the more fellows she had, she would feel like she was really something. I never thought about it that way. Girls like that, I guess they just felt they were making themselves the center of attraction, and not knowing they were really putting themselves down. They felt like, so what, it's going to happen. Most of them are messed up now, I think. Either they lost their virginity early, and because they lost their reputation, they don't care. A lot of them turned gay—they became lesbians because they were so much involved with fellows that no respectable guy would marry them.

The worst thing about being Puerto Rican is all the problems. There are problems in education, in employment, drug problems. The highest death rate occurs among Puerto Ricans and black addicts. Sometimes people won't employ you because Spanish people have trouble with language, and if you don't speak fluid English, you can't get jobs. I never really had trouble finding a job because I was never really looking for anything in particular. I just wanted a job. I was working in a bank for a while, and then I came upon Puerto Rican organizations. I applied because it was the area I grew up in, and I liked it. I want to go to school. I want to go to college. I don't know where. But now I can appreciate college.

When I first got out of high school, I didn't appreciate education. Then I didn't learn nothing whatsoever. Schools are the worst for Puerto Ricans. There is discrimination against Puerto Rican students, but it comes out in a very sly way. Being Puerto Rican, I was put in the worst classes. The guidance counselor was very negative about the whole thing. We didn't like that—not only me, but a lot of people. My friends, and like my brother. He wanted to go to medical school, but they said no, because they thought he wouldn't make it. Now my brother is a bacteriologist. He went to a college in the Bronx, and he still studies. I think my brother could have been a doctor. He wouldn't even have done as well as he did if he'd listened to what they told him. He was always interested in biology and science; he worked very hard. He got so far because he just ignored them. In fact he got angry and part of his attitude was that he would show them and that's what made him work a lot harder.

With me it was the other way around. I was disgusted. By the time I finished high school, I had enough. Before then, I figured maybe I would do more in school, but by the time I finished I was so disgusted I was just glad to be out. I figured if high school was like this, what would college be like? Sometimes I get angry because I think there was so much I could have learned. So much. Now I'm appreciating what I could have gotten, and that's why I'm thinking of going back to school.

I think most Puerto Ricans are scared to get out. They're just scared. I really don't know how to put it, but they should try to advance themselves. Instead of laying back and being scared of what may result from any action they take, they ought to go and find out. Like welfare cases, and various students and people. They ought to get out.

I really don't have any heroes. I never look back in the past because I wasn't there. Kennedy I admired. I think most of the Puerto Ricans did. And when he died, the reaction throughout the community of Puerto Ricans was remarkable. I was 12 and when we heard of his death, myself and a lot of other people started crying. I was in junior high school, and I remember most of us just crying. He was such a warm-hearted man, and we felt that he could have been someone who would have done something for us. That he was someone who looked at us like just people. I guess he just had that warm feeling, and that's why he won over most of the Puerto Ricans.

When I was younger I wasn't so proud of being Puerto Rican as I am now. Sometimes I was even ashamed, because of the way I spoke and the way people used to refer to me, like, "Oh, you're Puerto Rican. Wow." And when I'd go for a job some people, because of my last name, thought I was Italian. The same thing used to happen to my brother. And when we faced them, we could see the disappointment on their faces.

Puerto Ricans are thought of, I guess you could call it, as working people. They didn't make much money, but that's what I mean, they were really working people. Mothers and fathers trying to struggle up and bring their families up. Puerto Ricans are clean. I though I was clean cause of the way I was brought up, but so does everybody else feel that way. A Puerto Rican person wouldn't think of giving her child a half of a sandwich or keeping them on a bad diet like many other people might, whites or others. A Puerto Rican family—no matter what, they offered you.

I always think of Puerto Ricans as being friendly, yes and very nosy, always minding everybody else's business. Like now, I live in the Bronx and I like it. I wouldn't say it's more friendly, though. Like, in a Puerto Rican area if somebody is sick or something, there's alway's somebody you can count on. They'll help you out. They're your own kind. But not only that, they see your problems. But if you live in another area, people are sort of in their own apartments, and their own lives. Puerto Ricans are always in everybody else's house. Very personal things you always knew, like, "Oh, my daughter's in trouble." "My kid did this or that." They always talked about it with you, as one neighbor to another. Before you knew it, the whole building knew about it, and then the whole block knew about it. And a secret wasn't a secret anymore.

I always thought of Puerto Ricans as being very strict and very backward. The men were very strict with the children. At the time, that's the way I thought. Now I see the reasons for it. And families gathered a lot, always talking very loud. There would be holiday gatherings. New Year's was a big holiday. I guess the only thing special that bothered them was that there is a lot of crime, and people would talk about how much they had suffered. They didn't say much, but in one sentence they would say, "Let the coming year be nice, not like the past year," and they'd have a tear in their eye. And that means to anybody that the past year must have been a hell of a year.

Somebody says I'm Puerto Rican, I say I'm very proud about being Puerto Rican and I was always proud. I was proud because of the way I looked. I knew how to handle myself, I wasn't intelligent, but I wouldn't let anybody dare and pull anything over on me. I tried to make the best of things. And I could be proud of my parents. They gave me so much love. I was proud to be a Puerto Rican because that's my race and I have to live with it. I don't know what the message about being Puerto Rican is because I never was anything else. It's hard to say why it's good to be a Puerto Rican. I'm sort of accepting it because I am one, and not because there's anything good about it. I'm not saying that, if I was white, I wouldn't be better off. But if I could be born over, I would be a Puerto Rican again because of the things I learned. I grew up in a bad neighborhood and it made me experience a lot of things. But if I could go and do the same things over again, I'd do it exactly step by step even though I may have suffered a lot and had trouble. Because I've experienced so much and if I hadn't, I don't think my mind would be that wide.

THE SCHOLAR

My name is Joachim. When my parents came from Puerto Rico we were very poor. My father came here first, sort of to break ground and make a trail. And then he sent for my mother. When we first came here we lived in a good neighborhood and were the only Puerto Ricans. Everyone else was Jewish, and it was very hard for me to go to school. I had a lot of troubles and problems and I didn't speak the language. I didn't have any friends. I had no clothes and had to wear the same thing all the time. There were three kids in the family and we didn't have enough money. Today my father's worked his way up to the foreman in the shipping department, but in those days he was just a worker. And he wasn't making that much money— maybe about $40 a week.

I was picked on a lot and called different names. It was a good thing I could fight, because I really had to fight my way through school. All my friends were Italian and Irish then, and later, when the Puerto Ricans started coming in my school, they used to call me "Whitey." They were against me for hanging out with white kids; but if I started hanging out with Puerto Ricans, then my white friends wouldn't have talked to me. I think of myself as a white person. Black people, white people—they're the same. Everybody's got the same thing inside them. You got a heart, they got a heart too. We got feelings, they got feelings—we got blood, they got the same blood.

I had a Jewish teacher when I was 14 years old. Everytime she got mad at me, she said she'd send me back to Puerto Rico. That really upset me because I was born and raised here, not in Puerto Rico. I even went and spoke to the principal about it. But they believed the teacher, not me. When the teacher sent a letter to my mother, and my mother had to come to school, my mother believed the teacher too. And she hit me right in front of the class—in front of all the kids and my friends—but I was telling the truth.

Still, if it wasn't for that teacher, who was very strict, I would never have graduated high school and then gone on to graduate college afterwards. She wanted all of her students to get ahead, and I was the only Puerto Rican in the class. She worked extra hard on me. I wanted to quit school, especially because she was so strict and I couldn't stand her, but this teacher and my mother worked together. Every time I went to school this teacher would give me a letter which my mother had to sign at night, so I had to go—I couldn't cut. But I learned a lot from her. Those types of teachers you don't find nowadays.

When we were growing up we were poor, but we had real love in the family and it didn't matter. My mother, my father, my sisters and my brothers, we all of us loved each other and we were very close. Puerto Rican families are usually very united and also very strict. They feel something special for one another—for Puerto Ricans and Puerto Rico. And in Puerto Rico they feel even more for each other. But here they learn to be selfish and just think of themselves. We learn from Americans but we learn the wrong things. From the Americans we learn to want everything we see and we try to copy the Jones's.

Puerto Ricans have three different cultures. There's the African, Spanish and Indian and they all combine. The rhythm comes from the African music, the mannerisms come from the Spanish, and the food and way of dressing comes from the Indians. In Puerto Rico there are a lot of different towns named after the Indians. There's special food too, like rice and beans. But I've become accustomed to American food. In fact, I don't like Spanish food—I like Jewish food, and then I like Italian food.

Puerto Ricans are also very superstitious and Catholic. They're even more superstitious in America than in Puerto Rico. But here the Church has no influence on young people. They do whatever they want; they don't believe. But in Puerto Rico, John the Baptist is the favorite saint. In fact, he's the patron of the Islands. San Juan was named after him. And the virgin of Lourdes. Each part of the island has a different saint but John the Baptist is the main one.

Unfortunately, young Puerto Ricans don't know that much about Puerto Rico. I think it's bad for Puerto Rican kids growing up in urban areas today because it's so easy for them to get into trouble. Like me, I had to struggle to get where I wanted to be. Nobody really did anything for me; I had to do everything myself. Everything I know I found out on my own because I wanted to learn. They don't. I think ignorance is a bad thing. People should learn the culture and background of Puerto Rico and Puerto Ricans.

THE WOULD-BE MODEL

My name is Dorita. I live in an apartment house with my mother and father and my brother. My landlord is very sloppy. Like for example, I have problems with my door, getting into the apartment and then keeping it locked. It's not safe. My mother tells him, "Fix the door." And he says, "Yeah, yeah, I'll fix it tomorrow." So tomorrow comes and he doesn't do it and you've got to keep pressuring him and pushing him. Until finally you really get loud and in the end he fixes it.

I'm going to get out of this ghetto because I've seen too many things. When I was in the sixth grade I was coming home from school and the minute I got out of the elevator a man came up and grabbed me. I didn't know what was happening and I started screaming. I had to fight him off. He put his hand over my mouth and I bit it and he let go. I started screaming for my mother and running, but he ran after me and held me. I was halfway up the roof when the man let go of me. I don't want to live here any more.

I also want to take out my little sister. She's about six. We say she's my little sister, but she's really not. She lives upstairs, and her mother and my mother they're friends and call each other cousins. But I'm going to take her out with me when I leave because she's seen too much also. She comes upstairs and she tells me she's seen a guy take an overdose. She shouldn't know about that at her age. She could tell *you* everything.

Other things happen in this neighborhood. Many times when you're a girl and you're walking down the streets, the men look at you funny. Like when you're going to the movies the men stand on the streets. You get used to the way they look at you but you never like it. You just keep walking down the street, and no matter what they say, you don't listen. I don't dislike men. I judge people for what they are. Like the man who attacked me in the elevator. He was Puerto Rican I think, but I don't dislike Puerto Rican men because they're different from him. The same thing is true for blacks and whites or whatever groups. What one man does, I don't blame the others for it.

I like to go dancing but I don't like Latin music. It's too confusing. It's dumb. Because I'm Puerto Rican I had to learn it for the culture and everything. But I think I do better with soul. What people dance now is mostly soul. There's been more and more rock places now. Some people still do Latin but I don't like it and there's too much turns and things like that. I like soul.

I used to go with guys because I didn't want to be alone. I've had six or seven boyfriends and the nicest one is the one I'm going with now. The least nicest was the first guy I went out with. I went out with him and I used to like him but he used to treat me cold. He'd take me somewhere and he'd take care of me, but the way he used to be, I got so I didn't like him so much. So I let him go.

Next I was going out with a guy who was a junkie. When I started going out with him he wasn't, but he started smoking pot and stuff like that and he changed. He slapped me once, but I don't think there was any reason for it. He told me his friends needed cigarettes and he said let them smoke mine. I said, "No, you've got your own." And then he asked me again and when I said no again, he slapped me. So I slapped him back.

My last boyfriend was Peter. I didn't like him that much but I had nothing else to do so I saw him. He killed time. He would run up and down the streets with me in the summertime. We used to go to the park where the crowds gather. He liked me a lot and I don't like guys like that—if a guy likes you a lot he sometimes tries things. But Peter never tried anything. He was sort of sweet. I don't like guys who say, "Don't do this," and you can't do it. You tell me, "Don't do this" and I usually do it. He never told me what to do.

Before that I had a boyfriend who had a twin brother and I didn't know who was who. I used to walk up the street with my boyfriend and people used to tell me, "That's the other one." And I'd say to him, "Who are you?" And they used to confuse me back and forth. There was another boyfriend when I was thirteen. He became my boyfriend because my friends came back to me and said, "He likes you."

Some boys just like to get you and then drop you like mad. It's very hard now to find a good guy. Guys are either drug users or in Viet Nam or mixed up somewhere like that. There are guys all over the place who do all kinds of weird things. They like to go out with you just for the kicks. When I go out with a guy, though, I've got to know him for a long time. Usually guys who live around our way never go steady with anybody. They're just good guys.

I'm going steady now. His name is Joey. He looks more like a Greek than an Indian but I don't go out with him because he looks Greek. I'm not prejudiced. I don't care. If I like you and you like me—okay, I don't mind. He's okay because he doesn't treat me in a brutal way. There's a lot of guys who like to take advantage of you. They like to beat on you for any little thing. They tell you not to cross a street and you cross it anyway, and they'll slap you right away. He's very gentle and he doesn't lose his temper. He doesn't hit me. The way he treats me, it's nice. He understands me and I understand him.

In my house they tell it like it is. Like my mother sits me down and she says "You're going to school for yourself. You're not going to school for me. If you want to get out of Harlem, you've got to get yourself out, because I'm not going to get you out." But then she also tells me sometimes that I'm not going to make it. She tells me that I'm bad— but one of these days I'm going to hit her over the head because I really study hard and try. I'm going to be something she doesn't expect of me—I'm going to be a model. I want to go to modeling school. I'm also thinking of taking up bookkeeping.

I enjoy school but sometimes the teachers get on your back too much. They work you too hard. I don't mind a little homework but they give you so much homework—they pour so much on you and don't realize that you've got a lot of crap to come home to. Sometimes it gets me. I have enough problems.

There's a lot of trouble with drugs in school. They're all over the bathroom. People in bathrooms would be snorting, and they'd say to me, "Do you want some?" Like I've heard so many things about it—I've heard how people get sick and how they die from them. And I've talked to people who tell you they want to get off drugs but they can't. Some people, like my mother and father, they think I never stop to think about myself and my future. But I really do. I really understand. My brother is only thirteen, but he knows that he'd get beaten up if he did anything. When you hang around with guys, you can tell if they take stuff—their eyes get watery, they're never hungry, they get sloppy around you, eat candy and they're always nervous. They dress real sloppy. My brother hangs around with guys who do but I don't think he'll take it. I've been tempted to take it. Like today a guy I know comes up to me and he says, "I've got this stuff . . ." But I just kept looking at him and I said, "No." Because I know that if I did it once I might like it and do it again.

I think drugs are like losing your life. The more you take the worst it is for your body. So I never touch the stuff and I don't think I ever will. When I was younger, there used to be a lot of guys all over the place smoking pot in the hallways and doing other things all over the place. But as far as I know none in my family has ever taken it. And I think that's right. I'd never live with anybody who takes drugs. Once I took a puff of marijuana. It wasn't really even a puff—the person was still holding it. He still had it in his hand and it was up to the real smart part, the roach, and I just tried to get a taste out of it because I was curious to see what he got out of it. I didn't like it. It had a bad taste. I never tried it since. It didn't do anything for me. I really didn't like it. It tasted a little bit . . . oh, I don't know nothing about that, so I don't know.

I'm happy most of the time, but winter is not so good because in the winter, who is going to throw you in the water pump? Last summer was the first time I ever got thrown in the pump, and it was a lot of fun. They open up the pump and they play with these cans and they spray up, and the guys push you in the street and then they sit on you and you get soaking wet and it's beautiful. Everybody's sitting on a stoop. Everybody's friendly. Every day is like the fourth of July. And on the fourth of July you've got firecrackers—we go to China Town and we get shopping bags full of firecrackers. It's nice.

I like New Year's too, but everybody cries. I don't know why. My mother cries because she made another year or something. My sister cried and I said, "Why are you crying?" and she said, "I don't know." The only thing I got for Christmas was my coat and my ice skates. I really didn't want anything else. I didn't even expect them because I really wanted them last year—I didn't get anything for Christmas then.

I'd like to tell white people to stop and think and just give us people a chance. Like let's say you go somewhere and you're looking for a job, and the company is white. They don't even take a second look—they just don't give you a chance. There's a lot of Puerto Ricans who know plenty of things. They're pretty intelligent, but if you don't give them a chance, how can they prove themselves? Right now there's plenty of Puerto Rican guys and they could turn out to be lawyers and doctors. But when they see people discriminate against them, they won't even go to school. They stop and think, "Damn, what am I going to go for? I'll never make it big." That's what my friends say. We don't want to be a secretary—we want to make it big. But we say, "Why bother going to school? I'll never make it."

If white people wouldn't bother with me, I wouldn't bother with them. I wouldn't be snotty and rude to them or anything. I try to be friendly and if they tried to do anything to me, like curse me or something like that or called me spic, well there's a lot of people who are prejudiced. Not especially whites, but all races. You always find a lot of people that are prejudiced. I'm not—I can get along with blacks, whites, everyone. I have a couple of teachers that are white and I get along with them okay. Just as long as you understand each other, everything will be all right. But some people, you know, they meet a white person, right? And right away they give them these looks, like, "I can't stand you," or something. I'm not that way. I try to look at everybody the same way.

White people—let's say a Puerto Rican does something to them. And they see another Puerto Rican and they look upon them like they were the one who did something wrong. Like, some Puerto Rican kids, they go into trains and when they're ready to get off the train they smack people. White people just sit there and then they look around and they look at you like *you* did something. They make you feel bad when they look at you like that. Everybody is an individual. Puerto Ricans are better people than what people think they are—at least, some of them are.

I'm proud to be a Puerto Rican because I see what they're doing and I know what more they can do. I'm proud to have them as friends. Like my parents—I'm proud of having them as my parents. It's just something in me that you can't explain. The only thing about being Puerto Rican that I don't like is I don't like being discriminated against. Like right now you go up to the Bronx to a Jewish neighborhood and mostly these Jewish ladies, they give you these looks. Naughty looks. You think you'd like to get one of them—if I could get one, I'd kill them. Some people are like that. To me, everybody is equal. I'm glad I'm Puerto Rican. It's in you, you're Puerto Rican.

THE GANG MEMBER

My name is Carlos. I guess the worst thing I ever done in my life was to join a gang. But you can't not join a gang here because you need the protection. My gang's got two groups and there are forty-four of us. My cousin was the war counselor but I'm taking his place now for a while. While he's in the hospital. He got shot by another gang, and what they done to my cousin they gonna get worst from me. My cousin, his body is paralyzed now. He'll never walk again. He's coming out of the hospital in a few weeks and they'll have to carry him out. I want to see that guy who done it dead. I even got my gun ready. I've used the gun once at a cop, and I'm glad I missed him. I used it because he called me "spic." I don't like nobody to call me "spic," and I don't like nobody to curse at my mother or grandmother either.

I had my mini-bike in Central Park and I wasn't doing nothing and he was hassling me and said, "Move on, spic." So I get on my mini-bike and I start shooting wild as I rode away. Boy, I was angry. But I'm glad I missed, because if I hit him, they'd have come after me and hunted me like a dog. They would do to me worse than what they do to a dog because they'd beat me before they'd kill me.

I hate cops. I don't hate no Puerto Rican cops because they're my own people—but white cops and black cops, I despise them all. And I'm happy if a black cop or a white cop gets killed with the way they treat our people. I saw a lot of people with cracked heads from cops. I never got into trouble really because I'm cool. I want to keep my record clean. If you be arrested once, it's all over for you. To be cool, you look around, you don't go out when they've got action going, and you don't be friends with guys who get into trouble.

I don't need no cops because I got plenty of protection from my gang. If you're with a gang and you get hit, you're not alone. You've got friends who will help you and that's important. Most of the guys in the gang are Puerto Rican but there is a Negro, just one. But he's almost Spanish and he's as good as us because he was brought up in a Puerto Rican neighborhood. He can understand what we said because he grew up in a Puerto Rican environment. That's considered real good, when blacks hang out with Puerto Ricans since they were young and they pick up the language—it's like a little baby learning how to talk. They just catch on to what we're saying.

There's a lot of good guys in our gang. One of the top men in our gang was walking to the bus stop and these two guys caught him. They bashed his head in and broke his knee caps and threw him against a fire hydrant. They hit him over the head with pipes so he had like a hole in his head. He was in the hospital. He's all right now. They did it just because he was from another gang. I don't know if they wanted to kill him, but I think so the way they battered him. But I couldn't really say what they were thinking. I felt sad when I found out about it.

They caught one of the persons that did it. They beat him up with their hands and he was a mess. About nineteen of our guys came to get him and his friends and they started fighting with chains. I saw one guy hit another guy in the knee with a pipe and then the guy's brother stabbed the guy who was attacking his brother. It was a really terrible fight.

Later we fought them again. We decided to fight them in the park. It was supposed to be a fair fight, one to one, but it didn't end that way, because whenever those guys saw their man losing, getting beat up, they would join in and help him. They had baseball bats. When I saw all those baseball bats I got nervous. I thought, "What did I get myself into?" I didn't get hurt, though. But they had guns too. Two guys pulled up and shot one of the guys in my gang in the leg and paralyzed him for life. The guy who shot him went to jail, but he didn't go to jail for that. They caught him with dope— he was pushing dope and also stealing cars. He was one of the biggest car thieves around here.

I don't like this killing but I gotta admit I sometimes feel like killing somebody too. Once my brother got shot. He had an argument with someone and when he came back up to apologize, another guy came out of the kitchen and shot him in the head. My brother went to the hospital and they took two bullets out, but one is close to the temple and they can't operate cause if they make a mistake, he could die. So they just left it there. And then about a month after he came out of the hospital he got shot in the chest. I don't know why—I guess it had something to do with the gang again.

I once saw a girl get shot. She was playing a hockey game and all of a sudden ra-ta-ta-ta. There was this guy with a .38 on the roof. He had made a gun into a rifle. He was trying to shoot at a guy and she was in the way and got hurt. She died just standing there. She was about six years old. It was awful. Her brother came—she had a big brother. You know what a person looks like who's been shot? Blood all over. It looked awful, I'll tell you that much. They look cold and lots of blood pumping out. I felt sad. The family felt real sad. My mother came in crying. Her mother was crying and crazy. The brother came in with a knife and he wanted to kill the guy who shot her. They caught the guy with the rifle and brought him down. He said he was sorry, but that wasn't enough. It was an hour before the ambulance came, and it was too late and she died on the way. First I thought it was my own sister. I got scared—when I thought it was my own sister I was going crazy. The guy who shot her, he was sent to prison. Her brother with the knife, they held him back. He never got to him.

I'm glad I'm a Puerto Rican cause Whitey get everything thrown at them because they have everything. Like us and blacks, we don't have everything. I know my sports —my only Puerto Rican hero is Roberto Clemente. But there's no Puerto Rican football players. These whites think they've got everything. They think we can't get up to their class. If I had them all lined up in front of me I'd get a Tommy gun and shoot them all down, because of the way they're running the world. The Constitution says all the people are equal, right? Why don't they treat each other as equal then? They don't go by the Constitution. Some white people may be nice but not all white people. Everything is run by white you know. I never saw a Puerto Rican President or anything up there. A black —you never saw a black President. Americans have a habit of getting their nose everywhere. Like Vietnam. We can't get our boys home from there. Most of the boys that go over there to fight are Puerto Ricans and blacks. That's what I think.

Blacks are cool. They use the knowledge of helping the people. I like the Black Panther, Bobby Seale. He's cool. He's helping his people. That's what I like about him. He does more for his people. There's somebody like that for Puerto Ricans—he's a Young Lord. He's trying to organize because they want more help for their block. Because let me say this: a lot of Puerto Ricans work in factories, schools. By people helping, making better housing, better factories, things could be better. They want more money, man.

Puerto Ricans and niggers, they get along because they're fighting for the same goals. Fighting for more freedom, more opportunity to get a job. Depends on what area you live in. When I lived in Brooklyn, I lived down there ten years, we used to fight with a black kid every day—every time we used to go to school, playing or anything. They used to call us "spic," and I'd call them "Black Boy," and "monkey." Stupid names. But over here we don't fight. There's more of us Puerto Ricans, so what are you going to fight about?

The only thing different about being Puerto Rican

in school is maybe if you're Puerto Rican in high school, you didn't get the right diploma. They didn't want to give you right classes, the right opportunity or scholarships, maybe. They didn't think of you as going to college or wanting special programs. You didn't get a chance to get the right education.

Some of the white teachers give us a lot of shit, us Puerto Ricans. There's one man I hate. Because he's white, he thinks he's the head man of the whole school and I want to clip him. I'm dying to. But if you hit a teach you get suspended out of school. It gets on your record. I think he's prejudiced. I know that by the way he treat us. He bosses black and Puerto Rican kids and Chinese kids —those are the only people he bosses around. That teacher called me a Puerto Rican Jew once because I got a lot of friends who are Italian, and when they got problems, I help them, and when I got problems, they help me. So we stay together. I don't hate white people. I like them. I'm not against white people because they're people, they're human beings too. Puerto Ricans and blacks— their skins are black; Puerto Ricans' skins are black too. Our skins aren't white cause white is like a piece of paper. But they're only colors. You've got to help them too, right? A lot of whites are poor and so are blacks and Puerto Ricans.

I like to box and the only people I fight are white people. I feel sorry for them because when I fight with them and I get into that ring, nobody can beat me. I'll tell you that now. Sometimes the black people think that they're better than the Puerto Rican. Other people think they're the best. But nobody can be up to a Puerto Rican, neither white nor black. They won't make it.

One thing I don't like about Puerto Ricans though is that only about a few of them are quiet. The rest just don't know when to stop talking. And when they talk they become too loud, and they always have something to say. Try to talk to somebody, and they're always interrupting you. That's bad. It shows they're lacking in manners.

I'm not really ashamed of them. I've grown accustomed to them. It's that they're just not happy. Some people they have a mean mother—you know, or this and that. They can never be happy. So they have to use drugs or something to make them happy. I'm happy already so I don't need to take much drugs. People die when they take drugs. I seen guys in the corner puking, you know.

I see drugs in school—acid, cocaine, marijuana, glue. I smoke, but I get stomach aches from it. A lot of my friends take drugs though, because they want to be happy. Sometimes I get high with them. We smoke a lot on Saturdays—sometimes I feel so good then. I drink too, but I don't get drunk. Once I snorted dope. It felt so good—I forgot all my problems. But that night I had terrible pain in my stomach—terrible pains. So I stopped.

I tried acid. The best time was when I did it with a neighbor of mine and we spent the whole day laughing at each other. Like he'd keep moving his head back and forth and I'd see things coming out of his head. He looked like he grew a long beard, and long eyes and eyebrows. I stopped because, I don't know, I was afraid it was damaging my brain.

My friend got caught taking drugs in school once but I never got caught. I've gotten chased twice, but they don't remember who it was, they're too stupid. They think we look alike. Those teachers over there, they're stupid and they don't care for the students. They just treat you like animals.

In the 100% of kids going to school, 100% are cutting. Hardly nobody goes to school. Many are out taking drugs. Drugs could be gotten rid of in the city if they wanted to. But people are crooked. They buy the cops off. You read in the newspapers where they're investigating cops—that ain't true. They don't care.

This summer I met this chick and I went out with her a lot for seven months, but we had to quit then. Because she wanted so much. She'd come up to my house and want me to lay down with her and you know, my mother was there. And my mother used to be a teacher. She understands English. And my mother told me she was pissed. Sometimes we used to lay down together beneath the blankets with a bottle of beer and some cigarettes with the television on. Even though I don't look at it, I love it on. And then I'd fuck her.

Then there was this girl four years ago—she really liked me a lot. And I really had no interest in her. But she liked me and sometimes she would tell me she loved me. That's what got me wanting to keep away from her. Because I don't want to have nothing to do with love right now. Maybe later when I'm more mature and older. But this girl wouldn't break up with me. Then my friend told me at this party she was scheming out with a guy. The guy was feeling her all around. So there I went to her and she looked white, she was so scared. I wanted to clip her but I couldn't. I don't feel right hitting a girl. So I said to her, "I heard you were messing around with a guy?" And she said, "Yeah, I got down with him." And I said "Wha?" And after that I had nothing to do with her.

Then I once saw this chick in the hallway. A nice neat girl in hot pants or something. And I checked her out and she started looking at me and then we decided to go together. And we played around, felt each other up and stuff like that. And then I heard she was a whore— the biggest whore in school. And I told her I didn't want to see her anymore. And you should know that the only girls that I ever went out with were Puerto Ricans. No blacks, no whites.

I was about eleven years old the first time I tried to fuck. I really didn't know anything about it. First I started kissing her like you do when you're little. Then I tried to feel her, and then we tried to fuck but she was stopping me mainly cause she was scared. She was twelve. Then after that, I just dropped her. I don't really like to hang out with girls like that. They're double faced. And I happen to think too much of girls, too. Then later I had more fun.

I guess I first liked it with these other guys who used to go up to this girl's apartment and I'd go with them. She liked it because there were four or five boys—but one at a time, you know. We'd have a real party. My family didn't talk about sex much. One of my girlfriends had a kid at thirteen. When she told her parents they started fighting with her and said she'd have to leave school to support her kid. Now she's trying to get a job, and she leaves the kid with our family. I'm not the father of the baby. We know who the father is. He's rotten. He doesn't do anything. My father said he always knew it would happen. Her other sisters are going to get pregnant too. They never go to school—they stay out with their friends real late.

I want to marry a virgin. I want a girl who's healthy and can have my kids. And I want them to grow up decent. I want a good wife. A good son. A good family. It will be hard to find a decent girl—real hard, I tell you that. There are some good things about getting married. When you have kids and you are married there's somebody who after you go they'll carry on with what you're doing. Let's say you're not married, and you do this and that, and then after you're dead nobody knows who you are. But if you leave a son, then they'll say, "He had a son," and the son will tell them who you are.

My mother really understands me. She lets me bring girls up to my room. She's like a priest, you know—you can tell her confessions, like that's the way she is. She don't hit me like other people. They think I'm bad and hit the living life out of me. But my grandmother only hit me once because I started using nasty language, like you know "mother-fucker," and this and that. "Mother-fucker" got her mad. She said, "The next time you say the word, I'm going to beat you up like I've never done before." I felt like I wanted to clip her when she hit me. She hit me hard, man, and hit me so hard she sent me to the stove. I didn't say nothing to her though. I just went up to my room and listened to my records. And then I fell asleep and then I came out and apologized and so did she and everything was all right.

Once my father hit me. I have a little cousin and she's sort of mentally imbalanced and you're not supposed to leave the door open. And I left the door open once. And when my father found out my cousin went outside, he hit me. He hit me real hard. I don't see why.

My real father, I saw him twice in my entire life. I've got a picture of him. My mom says he's in the Marines. Now I think he got out, but I don't know because my mother gets money from the army. I guess he's in the army.

I don't think the people around here have more problems than other people. I don't think it's worst living here than living on Park Avenue. Living here is not different. But sometimes Puerto Ricans don't get no respect. I don't care what color I am. I could be white, black. I don't care. It doesn't matter except I got the same blood, Puerto Rican.

The color is what's special about being Puerto Rican. I don't know. I'm glad to be Puerto Rican. I've never been to Puerto Rico and I don't want to go. Because if I go over there I might stay over there. I'll go over there when I'm ready to stay over there. I want to stay there in a way because if you live over there, you've got some things you don't have over here. But I got lots of friends over here that I don't got there. I don't want to leave my friends. They treat me good. I wouldn't want to move away from here.

I go to church sometimes when I got problems. Like when I need money, I go to confession. And there I speak to the Father. I don't go into that box because I'm scared of it. I speak to the Father, and he tells me to say the Hail Mary five times, or say this thing twenty times, and he says, "God bless you and get out of here." Then I get money from my grandmother. The last time I prayed was when I wanted a girl back.

I believe in God but sometimes I have my doubts. I

have my doubts when I discuss these things with my brother and cousin. Like we were talking about this picture we saw about Jesus and the star—the star the Kings followed. It could have been a spaceship, that's why I have my doubts—because it could have been a meteorite or a spaceship.

THE FOSTER CHILD

MY NAME IS RAQUEL. I'm seventeen years old now and I was born in this country although my parents were born in Puerto Rico. I suppose they were okay when they lived there, but something happened when they came here. There were two children—I was the girl—and I have a brother. My mother was no good. She had a lot of men friends, and I guess we got in the way and she didn't want us. One day she packed up and left the two of us with my father. I've never seen her again since and don't want to.

We went on welfare but it was hard for my father to support and take care of us. Besides which, there's this Puerto Rican thing about boys—they're the ones that will carry on the line for a man and they're the one the fathers care for. So when my father had to get rid of at least one of us, it turned out to be me.

Until I was about twelve, I was sent to many foster homes. I don't remember very much of those years and I don't want to. Some of those people mistreated me, none of them loved me, and they took me only for the money.

The city pays a certain amount of money to people who take foster children, and some people take the money but don't do anything for the children with that money. None of mine, except one, meant anything to me, and I suppose I meant even less to them. They weren't homes to me, just houses and they were simply a place to sleep. I don't like to talk about it.

But one of the places, the last one I stayed in, was different. It was a Puerto Rican family and they really loved me. The strange thing is they had their own children too, but they treated me just like one of their own. I don't know whether they collected the city money for me, but they certainly spent more than their allotment on me. If they bought clothes for their own children, they would buy me clothes as well, and just as expensive. If my foster mother or father wanted to bring their children a present, there was always a present for me. They were also physically affectionate which was something I wasn't used to with my own father. They would kiss me and tell me they loved me and that I was just like their own child to them. Sometimes I would even call them "Mommy" and "Daddy."

But then one day the city took me away. I suppose they thought it best, since there was a home they could put me into where I could stay until I was twenty-one. I guess they decided that one permanent cold place was better than a lot of foster homes. My foster parents didn't want to give me up but they had to. Maybe with their own children they couldn't afford to keep me and pay everything for me if the city didn't help. Maybe they just couldn't fight the red tape—you know, when the city decides it's going to do something there isn't much you can do about it. I think part of it also was that they wanted to go back to Puerto Rico—they had often told me they would take me also, and the city probably wouldn't let them take me out of the country. I don't know; but I know they were as unhappy as I was when I was taken away to the home.

They came and visited at first, but visiting days were even worse than the days they didn't come. The whole family would come to see me and those days were so beautiful. But when they left I knew they were going to their home where I should be also. I would cry for days after they left and when they came back they would tell me that they had cried also. They said they were still working on getting me back but there was always "red tape," and they couldn't. After a while, I became so upset after they left that they didn't come back. It wasn't their decision. The Mother Superior told me that she had told them not to come back—in fact, she wouldn't let them back when they tried to come and see me. She felt it upset me too much and that I had to learn to adjust to my new home—if you could call it that. At first I didn't know why they hadn't returned and I felt very badly about that— I thought they weren't coming any more because they had decided they didn't love me any more, or maybe they got a new foster child. And then one day the Mother Superior told me why. I started screaming and saying that I would run away and find them. But that wasn't so easy. For one thing, we were watched pretty closely, and since they knew I wanted to run away, I was watched even more closely than the other children. Also, I had no money so it would have been hard for me to get very far, and the home was quite far from where the family lived.

That was another problem: I didn't know where that was —I knew it was a long ride from there to the home, but I wasn't sure exactly what neighborhood I had lived in and what their address was. I was only about eleven at the time, and had led a sheltered life with them. So I had no way to find them. It was a common name and I knew there were thousands of people in the city with that name. So I gave up.

I didn't like the home. It was a Catholic place and very strict. The Mother Superior had been made my legal guardian and we didn't get along. She was constantly trying to control my life and tell me what to do and make me do things I didn't want to do. From twelve to seventeen were very hard years but lately I realized I didn't have to do everything she told me to and I began to rebel. I suppose I was bitter. Maybe I still am. My needs were never respected. As a person I was unimportant to the Mother Superior—just one more child to take care of.

I've also had troubles with my own family. My father has never come back here to see me although I have called him a few times on the phone. But my brother has come to see me, but only because he wants something. He's into the drug scene pretty bad and comes to me when he needs money. I know what he needs it for, and I don't like to help him get drugs which will ultimately kill him but I really have no choice—if I don't give him the money, he'll go out and steal for it and then he'll be in real bad trouble. And so will the people he steals from. That bothers me too—that he may hurt innocent people. People who need dope can get pretty desperate if they don't get their own way, and my brother could become violent if he started a life of crime. So I give him money when he asks and I try to make believe to myself that the money is going to something other than drugs but I know I'm only fooling myself. I don't know which is worse: giving him money for buying drugs or not giving him money and forcing him to do something desperate to get it. I suppose the second is worse, so I'll keep giving the money.

Another thing that bothers me is that my father never seems to want me to go home. My brother says it's not a good place and he isn't there very much anyway. But still, it bothers me that he never comes and gets me—especially on holidays, when all the other kids get picked up by their families and taken to someone's home for Christmas and Easter. Puerto Rican families are close and they're all together whenever they can, but especially at holiday times. I don't even get a Christmas or birthday present from my father. I certainly don't get it from my brother. In fact, I give him a Christmas present—money to buy more drugs.

I guess I'm the quiet type. I count on myself. I know what I want. I rarely go out and never go out on dates. I don't like boys. I just sit in my room except for evenings when I work in a department store wrapping packages. They give me 20% off on my own clothes, but I never buy any. I guess you could say that I really don't have any friends, but I'm not too happy with Puerto Ricans. They're too revolutionary—they want to change the world and make everybody like them overnight. I don't really understand the political situation and I don't want to get involved until I understand the situation completely. Then maybe I'll join up with some of them, but not now. I'm not really a joiner. I don't believe in Catholicism although I was raised in a Catholic atmosphere in the home. I guess I don't believe in anything except a family, which I don't have. To a Puerto Rican, even a bad family is better than no family.

I have to stay here in the home until I'm 21. I despise it. The girls here are stupid and all they ever talk about is stupid things like parties or boys or music or makeup. I have no friends here because I hate the girls and they hate me. How can you talk about silly things with them all day?

I'm not doing too well in school either. I guess I get discouraged easily. If I take a test and can't answer the first few questions on it easily, I don't want to bother with the rest so I just turn in my paper. Besides which, I miss a lot of classes. It isn't my fault really, but my brother often comes to see me during the school days and I guess the Mother Superior doesn't want any junkie hanging around so she pulls me out of class quick to go and talk to him. Afterwards, I'm always too upset to concentrate on classes. I sit and think of how he's spending the money and what might happen to him if he doesn't get his drugs, or if he should take an overdose and die. He's my brother even though I don't like what he's doing.

And if he doesn't come to see me, sometimes I have to go and see him. A few times a week I get a call from someone in my neighborhood that my brother's in some kind of trouble, and I have to go out and find him and take care of him. When I come back then, I'm also too upset to work at school. I cut a lot of classes even when my brother isn't involved. I'm thinking seriously of dropping out.

My problems aren't as bad as some people's though. There was a girl in the home who has been my friend since

I was little. We both came in the same week and had something in common—you know, going around and meeting people. I never told her why I was there but she told me that her parents were in a mental hospital and that's why the state had sent her. She had no brothers or sisters to worry about or have them worry about her—she has no family. I've always tried to help her. Sometimes I complain about my brother and my problems, but it could be worse—I could have this girl's problems and have nobody.

My room and board is paid for by the city and I get some money from them besides along with my job. So money isn't a problem and I can save up quite a bit. Besides which, I don't waste money on clothes and makeup and silly things the way the other kids do here. I spend some of my money on phone calls. This year I decided I was going to find those foster parents again. It's been very hard because their name is very common and could be spelled in many ways. I bet I've called more than a thousand people in this state and now I'm making long distance calls to everyone by that name in Puerto Rico. Mother Superior finally gave me the address we were living in when they left me and I went to the post office, but they had moved and left no forwarding address. No one seems to know what happened to them. But I'll keep calling until I find them and can live with them again one day.

THE PHILOSOPHER

My name is José. I was nineteen when I got married.
When I quit school I was living with just my mother. She
didn't like the idea because in school I was doing pretty
good. I was, well, on the school honor roll and I had good
grades. But I just didn't like school. I got to the point—
well, I met a girl and, you know, I wanted to see more and
more of her so I stopped going to school.

We had a nice Puerto Rican wedding. I got married
in a church and it was a typical Puerto Rican celebration.
I had torches and a best man and two bridesmaids, a maid
of honor, the *madrina* and the *padirino* (the godmother
and the godfather), my mother, and my wife's parents.
We marched down the aisle, and took pictures. After that
we got to the hall. One of my relatives had a little band
and they provided the music. Everybody had a good time.
A lot of dancing, a lot of food, good music and a lot of
liquor.

We had about six or seven cars with the horns honking and the decorations on the cars. I don't know how

that custom originated, but when you see a Puerto Rican couple getting married, you see all that. I guess it's just, you know, the joy of expressing the festive aspects of it. They won't blow the horns before you get to the church, but after you get married. Then they'll ride around the girl's house where she used to live and they start honking the horn.

Even though I'm happy with my wife, I regret quitting school. I finished it up in night school. But I'm a social animal. I learned more in my 21 years on the streets than I ever did in school. This is true of most Puerto Ricans. First of all, you learn how to get along with people in the street, then in school you learn about the various problems that surround you. In school you more or less get outside these problems even though when you go back home you go back to the reality of poverty and poor housing and what have you. My mother's on welfare. Money was always a problem. As far as managing for whatever was needed in the house, welfare covered that. But for my social activities, money for me was hard to get, so I had to get a job.

I was about twelve years old when I got my first job. It was in a market and I used to be up at 5 o'clock in the morning to get there by 5:30. I worked for a Jewish guy and we used to push pushcarts till 8. And then I had to get to school by 8:30. I didn't mind the hours, but I didn't like having to go to sleep so early because my friends would hang out in the street all night and have fun but I had to go to sleep at 9 so I could be up by 5. Sometimes I didn't, but if I went out with them, I'd stay up all night and then just go right to work in the morning, then to school—and I'd be so tired and that pushcart was so heavy and I was a small kid anyway.

Actually before that I shined shoes, but I wasn't making much money at that. I made about $3 or $4 a day and it used to buy me a shirt or whatever clothing I liked. At that time I did a lot of shopping. I enjoyed looking nice and I felt a great sense of accomplishment at having money in my pocket. This was when I was less than twelve and my father was alive so I really didn't need so much money. But still, my father didn't like me to shine shoes and so I used to sneak out on Saturdays—he used to work in the factory—and so when he went to work, I'd take my little box and get back home before he did. People were nice to me when I shined shoes and if I worked all day I could make about $4. I was tired after that when I got home.

Then I also had a job butchering and another delivering newspapers when I was about thirteen or fourteen. I began delivering papers in the morning before I went to school. Again I'd get up about 5 in the morning, pick up the papers and deliver them. I earned about $10 a week and used to spend it on clothes.

Our apartment had four rooms and the kitchen didn't count so there were really three. All together there were seven of us in those four rooms. My mother, me, my two brothers and my sister. My mother slept in one room, my sister in another and I slept with my brothers in the living room. It was like being in the army. The building wasn't very clean and it was kind of old, you know. The ceilings were falling down. Sometimes we'd freeze—if you had a broken window you have to fix it yourself, and the cold air would come in until you got it fixed. But if you didn't have money, you couldn't buy a new pane for a while.

There were rats too and I remember I was very scared of them the way they would suddenly run out at you in the dark. The first time I saw a rat I was very young. It frightened me, but I helped my brother kill it that day, that first rat I ever saw. We killed it with a broom and a baseball bat. It ran and we ran and like we were chasing it but I remember being afraid that it would turn around and come after me. I guess I was about eight or nine years old at the time, maybe younger.

The neighborhoods were mainly Puerto Rican and black. The blacks and Puerto Ricans didn't get along and there were a lot of gangs. They had a black gang and a Puerto Rican gang and they would fight each other for territory. I was never in a gang but my brothers were. I learned from the streets that I wasn't the only one who was facing the same bad conditions—I found out that others in the group were in the same situation I was and we all had something in common. We had the culture, the ideas, our views, and our views toward other people. I learned that we were quite different from, say, a black person and a white person, and that our lifestyle as Puerto Ricans was quite different—we used to have our activities in Spanish—like Spanish music, jokes in Spanish, and the little sayings in Spanish.

Aside from our environment, we're a happy people. I feel lucky to be a Puerto Rican. In Puerto Rico there's no distinction between black and brown—you have all sorts of people, you have white, you have black, you have in-between, tan, what have you, and everybody respects everybody. They make no distinction because of color. And that really unites the people. It's a good thing. Over here you have too much prejudice.

I find there are many white people that are prejudiced even though they may insist that they're not. As a matter of fact I used to hang out with some white friends for a while and they used to make a distinction not only between the color of Puerto Ricans but between Puerto Ricans and blacks. They used to treat the blacks as inferiors. And so I stopped going around with their crowd, because I think they're wrong. As a matter of fact, I had a fight because of it.

One of them called me a "spic" and I called him a "crack," and then he said he wanted *me* to apologize to him. Of course I refused. So he said, "You want to fight me, spic, come on." It didn't really bother me that he called me a "spic." The fight really started because I called him a cracker.

I remember the first time someone called me a "spic." I was with my brother in a store and we were just sort of looking around. And then suddenly the owner—he was white—turns to us and shouts, "Get outa here you spics." And I didn't know what a spic was so I turned around to see who he was talking to and there was no one there. So I sort of realized that it had to do with us and that it wasn't a nice word, because my brother was like real cool and he just looked at the guy for a moment and then he spit on the counter. Then he grabbed my arm and we ran out.

Prejudice makes me mad and I'm very hard pressed to get mad. I hardly ever do. That's not true of most Puerto Ricans. In fact there are some Puerto Ricans who are too hot headed—you tell them something and they react very quick. In Puerto Rican society there is this concept about *machismo:* a man is a man, and no other man is more of a man than him. In a physical aspect, it means being able to protect yourself if it means fighting with someone. I'm hard to get mad at any man. But if I have to fight, I'll fight. And it's hard for me to back down from a fight. If I back down, I leave myself inside. And that's why I can't do it.

It's not only physical, it's sexual too, and it carries over to the way guys act with girls. I think that's true of everybody. And especially a young guy, he'll try to prove what a man he is before the crowd just to show off for a girl. I had a lot of girl friends. I was about eight or nine when I started going out with girls. I was about twelve when I discovered sex. Even though this girl and I never got to do anything, I managed to touch her. That's when I first felt the sexual sensations and all that. My parents never talked to me about sex and I wasn't taught anything about it in school either.

After I reached a certain age, maybe I was fourteen, my brothers told me about the possibility of having sex with a girl. We talked about getting her pregnant and they told me to beware of this. That was the only time. Talking about getting girls pregnant was seldom done among my friends. It wasn't a big fear. Plenty of the girls I knew did get pregnant. They were very young, like sixteen. They had a boy friend, they had sex, and they got pregnant. A lot of them just disappeared; some of them stayed with their parents and never got married at all.

Whites make it very difficult for a person to progress. For example, in school there were some Puerto Rican kids that didn't understand what the teacher was saying because they only spoke Spanish. But he said, "Well, I can't take time explaining to you and hold back the rest of the class." I felt that was wrong. But I've heard that remark several times, and when a kid doesn't understand something, this can be quite deterring to him. And we have a lot of people who come from over there in Puerto Rico and who sign contracts in English and have absolutely no idea what they're signing. So they're actually being fooled, and this is still going on very much.

But there will have to be a change because if there isn't, things are going to be bad. A lot of people will start objecting and it might become a real problem. There could be quite a bit of violence.

My opinion is that what the Puerto Ricans need is more guidance on the school level, better than what they're receiving now. That would enable them to make decisions for themselves. Let them know what's being offered. The task is to find better jobs, like in the anti-poverty programs—I know there are many Puerto Ricans that are eligible to be working in the anti-poverty structure and to determine Puerto Rican uses for the funds. But most of the positions are held by blacks. They're having problems with that and it can get to the point with Puerto Ricans and blacks fighting each other for community control.

Another problem here is drugs. The first time I learned about drugs was from my friends in school. I started hearing the word "drugs" more and more often when I was about thirteen. Me and my friends, like if they had a brother who had been involved with drugs they would mention it. Or like somebody would be pointing out, "You see that guy nodding off, well, he's high on drugs." I simply couldn't believe it at first, because nobody in my family took drugs.

But then a couple of friends of mine in my class were taking dope. Heroin. And they were taking it in school until they caught one of them, and the other guy, well, he just disappeared—all of a sudden he just stopped coming to school. And some of the guys on the block are taking drugs. We had a baseball team and some of the guys that were in it suddenly showed no more interest. I guess they were too busy getting involved with drugs. I have no idea why they did but I know little by little that they just got separated from the crowd. I guess they had to steal to support their habits, either from their families or anywhere they could get money.

In high school, some guys offered it to me and I knew what dope was. I knew that once you take dope, even though you only take it once, you automatically become addicted to it. And that stopped me from taking it. In school, in biology class, they told us about drugs, where they come from and what it does to the body. I believe that what they said was true, at least some of it was, but not all of it. For example, they said you become addicted to marijuana and that's not true.

Another problem here is with the whites who control things. We did a survey last summer of all the businesses in our area and we found that 99% of them were owned by people outside the community. What I would like to see is community-owned businesses so the circulation of money will remain in the community.

If there were a Puerto Rican corporation, a big

business, it would help, too. Puerto Ricans would look up to it and say they want to do that. You see, they don't have that mirror to look up to, and I believe that it's very important. A Puerto Rican who has made it is Herman Badillo, a Congressman. But a lot of Puerto Ricans are sad because the district he represents is not dominantly Puerto Rican and he hasn't been, well—I think there are several obstacles in his way and he is overpowered in whatever decision he might make. But I think Puerto Rican youths need an image to look up to. If they were in Puerto Rico it would be something different, but here, they can't relate to those who are already established.

The police don't really understand us either and they treat us differently from the way they treat other people. They harass—I've seen many cases in which a policeman will go up to a white person and just speak to him in general. They'll say "Mister," or "Ma'am, will you move please?" But the language he'd use with a Puerto Rican would be, "Get the fuck out of here—move your ass you spic." Cops have called me spic, as a matter of fact it was last summer. There was a pump open in the street and there was a detective in plain clothes and he was driving by. One of the kids put up a can to the pump and the water sprayed in his car. And he backed up and he said, "Comeoverhere." And the guy didn't want to, and started walking away. So the cop said, "Oh that's what you want me to do? Follow you so the rest of your spic friends can come and take me on."

So the cop takes out his gun and for no reason at all he says, "I just wish one of you would try something, I just wish you would." And these were very young little kids and everybody was looking out the window at this man doing all these things and taking out his gun for no reason at all—just to scare little kids.

The police are like that. If there's a crowd of white people they'd be very calm about it. But if there's a crowd of Puerto Ricans they'll just rush in and use dirty language. Even if your wife is there, or there are ladies there, he'll still use dirty language.

I'd like to hit a cop, but I wouldn't because I would come out losing—you always do when you fight them. I saw a situation last week when this guy was having a discussion with a cop, and he told him, "You think you're big," and "You swing your club because you have that badge and that gun." So the cop said, "Well, okay, I'll take you on without it." So he took off his gun and his badge and they went into the backyard and had a fight. The cop got his lip busted by the guy, but the guy got his face bashed in. I thought it was good for the cop to handle the situation in this way, but I wished the guy would have won.

I think police are good in some ways. They're civil servants. There might be a time when you'd thank them for saving your life or protecting you from a mugging. But as far as them relating to the people in a fellowship aspect, they're very poor at that. There are many who help fight drugs but there are others who are corrupt. I saw a cop bust this guy once, and I knew the guy was a dealer. I knew he had dope on him, and he had plenty of money on him too. And then suddenly the cop pulls into a hallway with this man and you can't see what's going on for a few seconds. And then the dealer walks out and the cop walks out, and they're both smiling and go in different directions.

And cops are always trying to stop people from opening the fire hydrants but I think it's beautiful to have open pumps. The little kids come out. . . . As a matter of fact, I think that when they open the pumps they should just close the street off. When I was a kid I remember I really enjoyed it when they opened the pump and the fellows used to grab each other and throw each other in it. It felt great. You get a can and open it up and start sprinkling water all over the place. It cools everything off and everybody enjoys it, even just looking out the window and watching the kids enjoying themselves. A lot of kids come out, all ages, even adults, clothes and all, and it's fun.

Sometimes if you get too close to it the water pressure is pretty strong and it can just knock you across the street. It happened to me but I didn't get hurt. It feels good to be wet, especially on a hot day, and to afterwards go and sit down on the bench and get dry. When you open a beer can and put it right down on the pump and it sprays and there's a house nearby, you might break the window. That's happened. Then the lady called the police. I don't blame them because I know I wouldn't like that either. But if you open pumps in a safe place there's nothing wrong with that.

Another thing that people sometimes purposely do in this neighborhood is start a fire. It certainly isn't difficult because the houses around here aren't worth anything— as a matter of fact, they'll go up in smoke like that if you just light a match to them. You have to understand it's not that the people don't like the firemen, but when they start a fire it's to show their anger, and when the firemen put it out, it's like putting out their anger. And that's why sometimes you have firemen getting rocks thrown at them. But it's not really showing an aggressiveness toward the fireman. It's just that the fire is a way of expressing their anger.

I sort of like this neighborhood, though, although the gang fights we used to have there would bother me. I saw a terrible gang fight once when I was looking out of my window. I saw a guy get his head blown off with a shot gun. I have no idea why that happened. These gangs must have been fighting over territory—you know, "Don't step on my territory and I won't go into yours." I was about ten years old then and I saw the impact when he got hit and I saw his shirt. It looked all red and it was so full of blood. Everybody who was fighting just froze. And a couple of guys from the other gang started shooting back. The police came and so'd the ambulance. I have no idea if he died or not.

Americans also don't understand that Puerto Ricans have some of their own holidays or respond differently to theirs. A lot of Puerto Rican women cry on New Years, but I have no idea why. I've seen a lot of them cry, though—just about 12 o'clock, when the New Year starts. Maybe they have old memories of the past year that aren't happy.

And we have the day of the Three Wise Kings, January 7th. Instead of giving the toys out like we do here on Christmas, they give them out on the seventh, which is the day the three kings went over to Jesus and brought Him His gifts.

There was never a Christmas when I didn't get anything but some Christmases there were things I wanted that I wasn't able to get. But it kind of wore off after a while. I was about fourteen and I started realizing things and I told my parents, "You don't have to give me anything if you don't want to." But they always came up with something. That was their generous Puerto Rican way.

The Puerto Rican is a festive cat, you know. He likes moving around and going to parties and everything like that. Singing and dancing—that's part of our culture. And a lot of young people grow up under this atmosphere. That's the way I grew up. And that's why so many of them drop out of school. It's much more fun to go to parties and sing and dance than go to school where you don't understand something and they don't speak your language.

Even though Puerto Rico is becoming, little by little, more Americanized, there is still the image of a Puerto Rican dressed in white clothes with a big straw hat. It's true we're diffcrent, but Americans really don't understand how. For example, I'm sure many Puerto Rican kids before they leave home in the morning for school say, "Bendicion, Mommy," which means, "Mother, bless me." And she would say in Spanish, "May God be with you." I've never heard that in English. Or when she comes home from work, you'd say, "Bendicion, Mommy." That's from Puerto Rico. Puerto Rican families are very close.

I know there are a lot of Spanish kids that like soul music better than Latin. And that shows too, I think, that as time goes by, they are more and more identifying with the blacks—not with white Americans but the blacks. I like soul music too.

I like this neighborhood, regardless of its problems,

because I like the people in it. The only other place I'd like to live is in the country. You get to feel kind of closed in in the city. I've been to Puerto Rico several times and it's very open. It's real nice country out there. But it's still not my style of life. The pace down there is kind of slow. Everybody takes a break in the afternoon and it's very quiet. But I think I could live in the country. That wouldn't be too quiet for me because I like the warm weather, and I like the cold weather too. But Puerto Rico is warm all year round. The worst part of living in the city is the apartment and all that during the winter.

But I guess I still like this neighborhood best. I don't like the drugs or the housing but I like the people. I don't mind if my son grows up in a neighborhood like this. I'd rather have him live down here and associate with his own kind of people than move to the suburbs where I know he will be pointed out as somebody different and he might eventually forget who he is.